Praise for *The Friendship Initiative*

When Amberly speaks, three things happen—and usually in this order: 1) People try to hold their bellies to keep them from shaking uncontrollably with laughter. (This is useless. Bellies shake. I've seen it.) 2) People lean forward to listen to eternal truths packaged in relatable stories. 3) People walk away changed by this encounter. When Amberly writes, it's the same. Amberly woos you into her world with words full of wit and wisdom. I believe she's just as amazed by God's offer of divine friendship as the day she first believed, and she invites us to learn about it in this book. I'm thankful Amberly put pen to paper. She's much more portable this way.

    —**Anita Renfroe**, comedian/author

Amberly Neese has a gift for celebrating the lighter side of life while sharing life-changing messages of hope and biblical truth. Having had the privilege of sharing the platform with her at a number of women's events, I just love Amberly's unique blend of humor and wisdom, which comes through on every page of this meaningful devotional. Every story and insight encourages and inspires the heart and mind, providing new perspectives on the way Jesus loves others.

    —**Shaunti Feldhahn**, best-selling author of *For Women Only*,
       The Kindness Challenge, and *Find Rest*

The Friendship Initiative *is a fresh and often humorous look at Jesus's example of building friendships, connections, and, ultimately, His Kingdom. If you are feeling disconnected from others or God, this devotional by my friend Amberly Neese (who, by the way, is the only person who could write a book with deep insight and the perfect amount of laugh-at-ourselves moments) provides just the encouragement—and kick in the pants—we all need.*

    —**Kathi Lipp**, best-selling author of *The Husband Project* and
       Clutter Free

THE
FRIENDSHIP
INITIATIVE

31 DAYS OF LOVING AND CONNECTING LIKE JESUS

AMBERLY NEESE

Abingdon Press | Nashville

The Friendship Initiative
31 Days of Loving and Connecting Like Jesus

Copyright © 2021 Abingdon Press
All rights reserved.

Library of Congress Control Number: 2020950677
ISBN 13: 978-1-7910-1591-6

21 22 23 24 25 26 27 28 29 30—10 9 8 7 6 5 4 3 2 1
MANUFACTURED IN THE UNITED STATES OF AMERICA

Dedication

This book is dedicated to my family—not because I am feeling pressure from every other author in history who has dedicated a book to their families, but because my family really are the reason I can write, speak, teach, travel, work, make audiences laugh, and come home to people I truly like (not just love). Thank you, Scott, Judah, and Josiah for your unwavering support and for being my favorite people on planet earth and for not selling me on eBay when I totally deserve it. I am also thankful for the others in my family who have loved me through eighties hair, my rebellious youth, and a million mistakes I have made along the way.

I also want to thank the hundreds of women's ministry leaders, pastors, retreat organizers, Aspire and Marriage Date Night tour partners, and event planners with whom I have had the honor of serving alongside. Do not grow weary in doing good, my friends.

Finally, this book is dedicated to Jesus, who initiated friendship with me over forty years ago. I was feeling disconnected and disheartened, and He spoke through neighbors who invited me to church, a Southern preacher who let me know that Jesus wanted to be my friend, and a smattering of believers who poured into me and served to remind me that a friendship with Jesus is the sweetest of all. Jesus, thank You for being my Savior, my Lord, and my Friend.

Contents

Introduction

Are you tired of going through the motions in your relationships and your faith? Are you hungry for ways to connect with others and the One who created you?

Today we all long for connection. Despite faster internet connections, better Wi-Fi hotspots, and more ways to stay connected than ever before, our lives still feel less and less connected. We desire healthy friendships but feel less equipped to make and foster them.

I have been there. My husband and I moved to a new community, leaving friends behind in another state. Despite our connections with friends online, we craved relationships with people we could do life with in person. Though we're certain of the faithfulness of God and convinced that He made us for community and connection with others, we quickly discovered that knowing we need connection and actually experiencing it are altogether different!

As I sought and nurtured new connections and relationships, I leaned hard into the teachings and example of Jesus; and I found so much practical help and encouragement that I wanted to share it with others. That desire led me to write two Bible studies and now this devotional book on the topic of connection and community. Those studies lay the foundation for what you'll find in the pages of this book.

In the first study, *The Belonging Project: Finding Your Tribe and Learning to Thrive*, I suggest that in order to flourish in biblical community, we must follow the "one anothers" in the New Testament—those verses in the Bible that include the words *one another* and give us direction for relating to others as Jesus modeled and taught, such as love one another, serve one another, strengthen one another, forgive one another. These actions are not always easy, especially if our hearts are not right or we run into challenging differences or conflict. So, in my second study, *Common Ground: Loving Others Despite Our Differences*, I explore how to navigate these challenges and live at peace with others despite our differences.

Now I'm excited to weave many of the insights of these two projects together in this devotional to address both heart and action—or what we might call motivation and perspiration—related to building better relationships following Jesus's example. Jesus did not just come into the world merely to be born and die on the cross (although that would have been more than enough). He lived for thirty-three years on this planet to set an example for us, pointing us to God and helping us understand what it means to live a life of love and service.

The Friendship Initiative is a thirty-one-day devotional journey to help us look more closely at how Jesus established and fostered relationships with others. As we look at his interactions with all kinds of people—the sick and the healthy, the disenfranchised and the privileged, the religious and the nonreligious, the outcasts and the insiders, the sinners and the pious—we will consider how we might follow His example to have deeper, more fulfilling relationships. By looking and listening to the heart of Jesus, we can begin to look more like Him in all our interactions with others—even in our conflicts— and draw closer to Him in the process.

On this thirty-one-day journey we will discover thirty-one practical keys for building relationships, which are identified at the beginning of each devotion. Each day includes a Scripture highlight, a Scripture reference for the full story, a short reading, and suggestions for reflection and prayer. I look forward to making this journey with you as we learn to love and connect like Jesus!

Blessings,

Amberly

A Parable about Connection

For my fiftieth birthday celebration, I had a crazy idea. While most of the people in my life celebrated their half-century birthday with a cruise, big party, or girls' weekend, I chose something a bit off the beaten path—hiking the Grand Canyon. Though I live in Arizona and have visited the massive and beautiful tourist destination, I had never before trekked into the canyon itself. Even crazier, I invited others to go with me, and a handful of folks subjected themselves to training, cold weather, and hotel fees to join me on my adventure.

My birthday adventure companions included four strong and beautiful women who are part of a group I meet with monthly to connect with and pray for one another. I truly love and admire these ladies. I know that they are women who are fierce about prayer, but I had no idea how serious they are about hiking—until we started our trek. These beauties left my husband, nephews, and me in the dust! It seemed that every time we arrived at the next rest stop, they were just leaving. My idea that we would all hike together was proven unrealistic because of my slow and deliberate pace and their incredible cardiovascular health. As the distance between us grew, so did my sense of disconnection.

But then something wonderful happened to change my perspective.

When we had arrived at the canyon that morning, one of the ladies—the guide for the day—had given me a birthday "crown" made of felt with brightly colored candles on it. Despite the fact that I looked ridiculous with it on my head, I wore that hat on the whole journey. I knew it was a thoughtful gesture, but what I did not know was the attention that it would draw.

You see, because I wore that hat announcing my birthday, I had at least thirty people wish me a happy birthday along the trail. And because the Grand Canyon attracts people from all over the world, people from all walks of life were wishing me happy birthday in different languages. Because of my crazy cranial accessory, I was able to connect with so many beautiful and diverse people I otherwise would have simply passed on the path. But instead we exchanged greetings and smiles and love.

Eventually I was able to reconnect with my friends on the hike and enjoy being together, but not before I recognized how *blessed* I was to make so many other connections that day in addition to those with my friends. Often we have a certain idea about what connection and community should look like, and we wind up missing out on the blessing of the ordinary, everyday connections that are right in front of us. God wants to bless us through all kinds of connections and opportunities for community—from casual interactions to acquaintances to friendships. When it comes to loving and connecting like Jesus, we must keep our eyes and hearts open to all of the people He brings across our path each and every day. Just as in Jesus's life, sometimes the most significant interactions and even relationships begin as connections with others "along the road."

DAY 1
Grace Space

The Adulterous Woman

🔑 EXERCISE GRACE

Then Jesus stood up again and said to the woman, "Where are your accusers? Didn't even one of them condemn you?"

"No, Lord," she said.

And Jesus said, "Neither do I. Go and sin no more."

John 8:10-11

Read John 8:1-11.

This story unfolds like an epic Hollywood blockbuster with a soundtrack by John Williams. It is a story of betrayal and forgiveness, with a side order of judgment but a climax of grace.

Like the religious leaders in this story, I have viewed others with judgmental eyes before. When I am on a diet and someone enjoys a donut in front of me, my inner Pharisee comes out and I want to hit that person with a stone (hypothetically, of course).

This woman was dragged through the streets by religious leaders for all to see, with little clothing and even less dignity. They threw her at the feet of Jesus. She was aware of the weight of her indiscretion, but perhaps unaware that she was merely a pawn in their plot against Him. I wonder if she tried to cover her nakedness. Did the sneers from the surrounding crowd fill her ears, or did the pounding of her heart drown it all out?

The Pharisees wanted to trap Jesus, so they posed an impossible question—or at least they thought it was. What should be done to the woman? If Jesus agreed with the Law that she be stoned, then He would lose credibility with the crowd for being a person of love and mercy and grace. But if He said to let her go, then He made a mockery of the Law, which the Jewish people held dear.

Against a backdrop of chaos thick with anticipation, Jesus remained calm and silent. Rather than answer them, He bent down and started drawing in the sand. Why? Maybe He was trying to look into the woman's eyes to reassure her. Perhaps He was writing down the sins of the Pharisees. Or maybe He wanted to draw attention away from the woman so she could try to cover up. Whatever the reason, it made the religious leaders angry. They kept pestering Him until He spoke—and then they wished He hadn't.

"Let any one of you who is without sin be the first to throw a stone at her" (v. 7 NIV).

The stones that the religious leaders had picked up to throw at her began to fall one by one, beginning with the eldest man. These religious leaders, obsessed with outward appearance and status, dropped their facades and the stones and then walked away.

Jesus had saved her life and she knew it. Maybe that is why she addressed him as "Lord" when He spoke to her.

Jesus chose grace. As the only One without sin, He had every right to condemn her, but instead He reached out in mercy and kindness. He encouraged her to leave her old life behind: "Go now and leave your life of sin" (v. 11 NIV). I don't know what happened to that woman, but I do know she was never the same. Because any time you encounter Jesus, you are changed.

We can extend grace to others like Jesus did by coming alongside them and encouraging them to live a life of freedom and holiness in Christ. The world heaps plenty of shame and guilt, along with a side helping of inadequacy and insecurity. And we heap plenty on ourselves. What our friends need is a voice of love and kindness, pointing us to the grace and forgiveness found in Jesus.

> **What our friends need is a voice of love and kindness, pointing us to the grace and forgiveness found in Jesus.**

For Reflection and Prayer

- When was the last time you felt the disapproval of another? How did you want to be treated in that instance?
- Although the Scripture never mentions her name, Bible scholars titled her story "the Adulterous Woman" instead of "A Life Saved" or "Grace Experienced." If your story was written in the Bible, what would you want the title to be?
- Is there someone who has felt the sting of your disapproval with whom you need to reconnect and apologize? Remember, this does not mean you approve of this person's choices, but it can mean that you value her or him as someone God has created in His image.

Lord, help me see people and extend grace as You do. Make me aware when I cast judging eyes on those around me. Remind me of the grace You have extended to me over and over and allow me to show that same grace to others. Amen.

DAY 2
So Many Questions

Nicodemus

⚷ DISPLAY CURIOSITY

"What do you mean?" exclaimed Nicodemus. "How can an old man go back into his mother's womb and be born again?"

Jesus replied, "I assure you, no one can enter the Kingdom of God without being born of water and the Spirit."

John 3:4-5

Read John 3:1-21.

I love to ask questions. To some, that may seem nosy, but people are just so interesting. I love finding out new things from new people. Questions are invaluable tools. They are like

5

> **Questions are invaluable tools. They are like permission slips that allow people to share their stories.**

permission slips that allow people to share their stories, talk about their passions, and give insight into their pain. They can reveal what's in a person's heart, sometimes without that person even knowing it.

Nicodemus, a religious leader in his day, was accustomed to answering people's questions. I am sure his day consisted of people seeking answers and insight from him. Perhaps he felt like a CPA in April—everyone wanting a piece of his brainpower and knowledge. Except his seekers wanted to discuss God and the religious law, because he had studied and practiced devout adherence to the Hebrew Scriptures and was surrounded by other great religious minds.

But Jesus perplexed him. The signs Jesus performed proved that He was from God, but He did not fit into Nicodemus's understanding. Jesus looked and acted nothing like the promised Messiah—or at least what the religious leaders thought he would look like. They expected the Messiah to be more like them—pious and proper. Yet Jesus hung out with children, women, prostitutes, tax collectors, fishermen, and the poor and ill. He was born humbly and lived without pretense. He did not ask for recognition. He just wanted to point people to God.

Nicodemus had questions for Jesus, but why seek Him out at night? It's possible that going to visit Jesus would reflect poorly on this religious leader who was supposed to have all the answers. The other members of the Jewish ruling council might look down upon his desire to seek answers from the Jewish carpenter. Or perhaps he was afraid of being seen with Jesus, who was ridiculed by the other religious leaders. In any case, he went at night, under the veil of darkness, to speak to Jesus.

Nicodemus had questions—no doubt, more questions than are recorded for us. But the answers Jesus gave for the ones we find in John's Gospel are some of the most quoted verses in the Bible. I love that Jesus didn't get frustrated with the questions, nor did He condemn Nicodemus for failing to grasp His answers. After all, how can a person be born twice? You can't—unless you're not talking about a physical birth.

John, the man who wrote the Gospel bearing his name, didn't tell us how this nighttime conversation ended. But we do know that the encounter had an impact on Nicodemus. After Jesus's crucifixion, Nicodemus "brought a mixture of myrrh and aloes, about seventy-five pounds" (John 19:39 NIV) and helped Joseph of Arimathea prepare Jesus's body for burial according to Jewish customs of the day. Something had compelled Nicodemus to offer such an expensive gift for a burial, and I doubt anyone would be that generous to someone he or she didn't know or care about.

The questions Nicodemus asked bridged a relationship with Jesus and helped him gain a deeper understanding of God. Our questions can help us to do the same. When we cannot grasp what the Scripture says or what the Holy Spirit is saying, we can take our questions to God. After all, that's what we do in a relationship with another person. Why should a relationship with God be any different?

For Reflection and Prayer

- If you could ask Jesus any question, what would it be?
- Is there something in your life you need to bring into the light? A decision, relationship, sin pattern, behavior, habit, or question that you need to take to Jesus?
- Is there someone in your life you need to give the opportunity to ask spiritual questions? How can you provide an opportunity or open door?

Lord, You know my heart. Please help me sort through its contents for any questions I might have, and give me the courage to bring them to You. If anything in my life does not glorify You, Lord, let me bring it into the light so that I may walk in freedom. And when others have questions, help me to point them to You. Amen.

DAY 3
Going Out on a Limb

Zaccheus

[Zaccheus] tried to get a look at Jesus, but he was too short to see over the crowd. So he ran ahead and climbed a sycamore-fig tree beside the road, for Jesus was going to pass that way.

Luke 19:3-4

Read Luke 19:1-9.

As a ridiculously tall woman, I have always wanted to be shorter. In high school, all the basketball players I liked would date these pint-sized girls, short and sweet. I know there are advantages to being tall (all my kitchen cabinets are accessible, and I can look a giraffe in the eyes), but I am still jealous of my height-challenged friends.

Zacchaeus may have been short (v. 3), but his bank account was not. He was a tax collector, an unsavory job in the eyes of most, but a lucrative one nonetheless. The job entailed collecting taxes, often from those who did not have enough, enforcing tax hikes, skimming off the top, and losing friends in the process. Tax collecting was a very isolating job and it was considered a seedy one.

His status did not deter him from hearing about Jesus. His height did not stop him from doing everything possible (even climbing a tall tree) to see the Messiah. His wealth did not stop him from maximizing the short time (no pun intended) Jesus had in Jericho to connect.

Jesus did not let obstacles stop him either. He did not listen to the culture that looked down on tax collectors (verse 7 said "the people were displeased"). He did not give preferential treatment to those who got to the city early to see Him. Jesus knew Zacchaeus was in that tree, hungry to see Him, so He invited himself to the house of the tax collector and ordered him to come down.

I was at an event many years ago where comedian and actor Robin Williams was speaking to a group of kids. I was over the moon that I might have the chance to meet him. I parked in front of the stage door and rehearsed how the conversation would go, fantasizing that, somehow, I would make him laugh or that we would laugh together at something (have I mentioned that I suffer from chronic nerditis?). I waited a long time outside the venue in the direct sun for a chance to shake his hand. I had to use the restroom but refused to leave my place in line for fear I might miss the chance to meet the comedic icon.

Robin (we were on a first-name basis, you know) connected well with the audience inside the venue; I could hear the laughter through the seal of the stage door. However, when he came out, it felt like someone had unplugged him. He frowned at the sight of the line that had formed outside the door and did not even make eye contact with me, his biggest fan. All the lines I had rehearsed in my head were reduced to nervous mumbles when I finally spoke to him. I have to admit I was disappointed at how the encounter unfolded.

It was an entirely different story with Zacchaeus. He had wanted to see a glimpse of Jesus so much that he would run ahead of the crowd and shimmy up a sycamore tree. I can picture kids doing that, but not a grown man. And his efforts paid off—so much more than he probably expected.

Jesus knew Zacchaeus's name. Jesus called him out of the tree. Jesus went to his house. Jesus ignored the whispers of those around him regarding Zacchaeus's employment, and it changed Zacchaeus forever. He did not get an autograph, but he got something better: a new purpose. He promised to give away half of his possessions to the poor and make right any wrongdoings.

> **When we go out on a limb to connect with someone else, the benefits far outweigh the risks.**

These two men did not allow obstacles to stop a friendship from forming. Nor should we. With all the demands on our time, developing deep friendships can be challenging. We may have to overcome insecurity or awkwardness. We may have to meet before work or online. We will have to risk being vulnerable and open. But when we go out on a limb (pun intended) to connect with someone else, the benefits far outweigh the risks.

For Reflection and Prayer

- Who has overcome obstacles to form a relationship with you?
- What fears keep you from reaching out to form genuine friendships?
- What do you see as obstacles in your relationship with Jesus?
- What does this story tell you about God's desire for a friendship with you?

Lord, thank you for pursuing a friendship with me. Give me the same determination to develop friendships with others. Allow me to see those around me who need a friend. God, make me aware of the hurts of others that make them leery of friendships. May I never be deterred from connecting with others because of obstacles. Amen.

DAY 4
Truth Be Told

Pontius Pilate

O━┳ BE TRUTHFUL

Pilate said, "So you are a king?"

Jesus responded, "You say I am a king. Actually, I was born and came into the world to testify to the truth. All who love the truth recognize that what I say is true."

John 18:37

Read John 18:28-40.

The truth hurts.

When a boy in high school told me that he thought my sister was prettier than I was, it hurt. When I earned my first B in school (I remember it clearly), it hurt. When my parents told my sister and me they were splitting up, it hurt. When I received my first speeding ticket, it hurt—both my pride and my insurance premium. When I struck out the first time in softball, it hurt. When I recently lost a job I loved, it hurt.

We face painful truths every day—getting on the scale, paying taxes, trying on bathing suits, looking in a mirror at one's wrinkles, and receiving an AARP postcard in the mail, even if it was addressed to the previous owner.

It also hurts to tell the truth. It hurt to tell my family that my father had passed away. It hurt to tell a congregation we loved that we felt called to another one. It hurt to tell our kids when we hit a rough spot financially. It hurt to tell my parents that we had miscarried—again.

When attending a funeral one day, I had to face the hard truth—I was still bitter at the pastor conducting the service, who had caused hurt in the life of someone I care about. I had brought my daughter, Judah, with me to the funeral to honor the incredible woman of God who had died, and I did not want my sweet daughter to know how I felt about the pastor.

I thought I might not have to see this man, but wouldn't you know, just as we were entering the sanctuary, he came around the corner. We exchanged pleasantries, and then Judah and I sat down to participate in the celebration of life.

When we got in the car after the service, my perceptive daughter, who was around ten at the time, said, "You know, Mom, you have a 'tell' when you lie."

"What is a 'tell'?" I asked.

"A signal or gesture that you make involuntarily," she responded.

"I do not!" I retorted indignantly. "Wait, when did I lie?"

"When you saw the pastor. When you said, 'It is nice to see you,' you closed your eyes."

Busted.

Sheepishly, I asked a follow-up question. "Do you think he noticed?"

"I don't think so, Mom. He was too busy closing his eyes when he said it was nice to see you, too."

Sometimes we avoid the truth because it is uncomfortable.

When Jesus went before Pilate, both men clearly understood the gravity of truth and the pain it could bring.

Pilate was attempting to preserve his position and avoid sentencing Jesus to death. He wanted to save his job and avoid conflict with the religious leaders. He also wanted to please the crowd, and that desire swayed his decision.

Jesus's life was on the line, but He wanted truth to prevail, even if it meant His life.

The two men asked each other questions in this verbal sparring match. Pilate was curious on some levels, probably because his wife had told him of her disturbing dream about Jesus. Pilate didn't understand why Jesus had caused such a stir among the Jewish people, so he was to trying to decide if Jesus had done anything worthy of crucifixion.

On the other hand, Jesus used this opportunity to bring glory to His Father and proclaim the Kingdom. In sharp contrast to Pilate shying away from discomfort, Jesus leaned into it and spoke the truth. The hard truth. His mission came from a Higher Authority than Pilate could ever understand. Jesus came to "testify to the truth"—all the while, Pilate was just trying to save his own bacon.

In the end, Jesus's candor led Pilate to ask one of the most powerful questions in Scripture: "What is truth?" (John 18:38). The problem was, Pilate didn't realize that standing before him was "the way, the truth, and the life" (John 14:6). Pilate missed the answer to his own question because he didn't recognize the Source of truth.

Sometimes, we miss truth because we are too prideful to ask, too concerned with our own agenda, too unwilling to be uncomfortable, or too busy to get to the source of it. Pilate seems to have been a little bit of all of those things despite the fact that Jesus—the great fulfillment of truth, God's Word made flesh—was right in front of him.

Jesus, who is Truth, calls us to seek and speak truth in love. Truth spoken without love brings injury, but truth spoken in love with genuine care and concern for the other can bring healing and intimacy. When we care for others well, it is reflected in how we act, how we serve, and how we lovingly speak truth, even when the truth is hard to hear or hard to say.

> **Truth spoken in love with genuine care and concern for the other can bring healing and intimacy.**

I often wonder if Pilate would have accepted and heard truth more completely if he knew the depth of Jesus's love for him and the rest of humanity. If he knew the man before him was going to die for him (and every other sinner), would he have heard the hard truth more easily?

If we are to initiate friendships after the example of Jesus and serve others as He did, may we love others so well that they choose to allow the truth to set them free.

For Reflection and Prayer

- When do you find it difficult to tell the truth?
- What was it like for someone to speak truth to you when you didn't want to hear it?
- Is there someone with whom you need to share the truth in love? What holds you back from speaking truth in love?

Truth Be Told

Lord, thank You for being Truth. Thank You for sending your Son to show us the truth and calling us to share the truth with others in love, even when it is not comfortable. May my desire to please You and walk in Your truth and love always be greater than my desire to please others. Amen.

DAY 5
Out to Lunch

A Boy with Loaves and Fish

Then Andrew, Simon Peter's brother, spoke up. "There's a young boy here with five barley loaves and two fish. But what good is that with this huge crowd?"

John 6:8-9

Read John 6:5-13.

I may have to forfeit my "Best Mom Ever" coffee mug. My two kids have a favorite type of ramen (dry noodles) that they enjoy, and this afternoon, I discovered that there was only one package left. Normally, I am on some diet that makes me grumpy and won't allow me to consume empty carbs. But today I threw caution to the wind and ate the whole thing. I hid the empty package so the kids would not be any the wiser, cleaned the kitchen as if I was preparing for the health inspector, and smiled all afternoon with a Cheshire cat grin on my carb-loaded face.

Of all my heroes in the Bible, the boy who shared his lunch may be my favorite. First of all, he shared food. In my book, this is a very philanthropic gesture. Food sharing is the mark of a true friendship. We share in my family. If we order at a restaurant, we usually order different things knowing that we will have the chance to nosh on bites from the other plates at the table.

Second, the boy gave all he had. Generosity is admirable on its own, but when you couple that with the food thing, that is downright sainthood material in my book. He did not understand how giving up some bread and fish could help, but he was willing to do it anyway. I like this guy and his faith!

Notice that the little guy didn't ask what was in it for him or expect anything in return. He just shared. He just trusted. He just gave. He was selfless. He didn't eat first and then donate the leftovers. This concept is very convicting to me when the offering plate is passed at my church; I feel super comfortable giving God a portion of my leftovers, but am I ready to give Him all my fish and loaves?

Because of the boy's willingness to share, thousands were blessed that day. Because he was willing to open his lunch pail, a multitude of men, women, and children were able to open their ears to the message of hope that Jesus was sharing. Because he was willing to share his few fish, people's bellies were filled and they were able to listen to the One who called some of His followers to be "fishers of men." Because he was willing to sacrifice a handful of bread, hungry people were able to experience teaching from "The Bread of Life."

Let us not forget that the boy, too, was part of that crowd. He gave a small offering of fish and bread but received a benefit from the multiplication of that food way larger than his initial lunchbox contents. He left full both spiritually and physically, having heard Jesus teach and seen Him do extraordinary things with ordinary ingredients. God repaid his willingness to share with blessing. Thousands of years later, we are still talking about this young man. Although we never learn his name, we can surely benefit from his example of kindness and generosity.

Sharing is a vital part of friendship. Although sometimes it is about material items, often it has nothing to do with the tangible. Some of the most meaningful sharing we can do is intangible. If we are willing to share our lives, our schedules, our stories, our vulnerabilities, our hearts, and

> **Some of the most meaningful sharing we can do is intangible.**

our listening ear, we can indeed bless others. Whether it comes in the form of a casserole or a carpool, a hug or a helping hand, God can use our sharing in mighty ways to display His love. And like the boy willing to share his lunch on that day so long ago, God can use our sharing to satisfy the spiritual hunger of those around us, blessing us also in the process.

For Reflection and Prayer

- How are you like the boy who shared his lunch?
- Which of the boy's traits would you like God to increase in your life?
- Who has been an example of generosity for you?
- Who needs something you can give—time, attention, money, even a meal?

Lord, give me a heart like Yours—one that gives generously and loves gracefully. Show me how I can be more generous to share what I can offer, even if it seems small. Help me put selfishness aside and trust in Your provision. Amen.

DAY 6
Be Faithful

The Centurion

⚷ INTERCEDE FOR OTHERS

When Jesus heard this, he was amazed. Turning to the crowd that was following him, he said, "I tell you, I haven't seen faith like this in all Israel!" And when the officer's friends returned to his house, they found the slave completely healed.

Luke 7:9-10

Read Luke 7:1-10.

We own some knives. For only four of us in the house, we have a disproportionate number of kitchen knives in our house. We are not planning for the zombie apocalypse; we just love to cook and want the right tool (or twelve) for the job.

My mom and dad got a really nice set of knives when they got married. Those knives are still going strong, long after the marriage petered out. When Scott and I got married, I wanted the same type of knives to start our lives together. Scott came from a family where you just use cheap knives until they stop cutting well, and then you use them a little longer. When the salesperson came to our house (yep, that was a thing before the internet and Home Shopping Network), Scott was impressed with the demonstration, but he was not prepared for the astronomical prices of these kitchen tools. When he saw the price sheet, all color drained from his face. I thought he was going to throw up on the lap of the sales associate. After much discussion, cajoling, prayer, and compromise, we finally purchased a small set. Over the years, we have added to the collection, had them sharpened (they have a lifetime warranty), and even "lost" one of them at a church potluck. (If only there was a "lost and found" for church potluck items, right?)

Recently, Scott took our set to be sharpened. I had made the appointment online, so I used my cell number to make the appointment. While he was there, the slick salesman also tried selling him a new knife that had just been introduced. My husband said it was downright gorgeous, "but we do not have the budget for that right now," so the salesman dropped the subject.

A few days later, the salesman sent a follow-up text to my husband, not knowing it was my cell phone number, not knowing that he was putting his life on the line when he wrote: "Has the boss decided yet?"

> **Are you willing to put aside your pride, roll up your sleeves, and stand in the gap for another?**

Excuse me? I am the boss in this scenario? It was not a harmless remark to me. I wanted to punch him in the neck, but I understand the idea that in sales and in life, it is usually most effective to go to the one with the power.

The centurion in our reading today had the same idea—go to the one with the power. This man, a respected member of society in Capernaum, had a slave who was quite ill. This centurion had the insight to send others to ask Jesus to heal the slave. He also had the faith to understand that Jesus did not even need to be in the presence of the sick slave to heal him.

The centurion knew two things: his slave needed help and Jesus could heal people. The military leader put his reputation and his standing on the line by interceding on behalf of the sick man. He went to Jesus when his slave could not.

Are you like the centurion? Do you have people you advocate for on their behalf? Do you have people you pray for regularly? Do you have friends and family whose best interest you're willing to work for and defend? Are you willing to put aside your pride, roll up your sleeves, and stand in the gap for another?

If I'm at a restaurant with others and my order is not right, I am not excited about talking to the waiter or waitress in order to make it right. That being said, if someone else in the party has an order that is incorrect, I cajole them into talking to the wait staff member; and if they are not willing to speak up for themselves, I often take the initiative to ensure that the wrong is righted. I am a pushy broad, but especially when it comes to food!

I want to be like the centurion. I want to be willing to stand in the gap for my friends (not just when their steak is not cooked properly), to ask Jesus to work in their lives, and to go to Jesus when they cannot. That is not only an expression of faith but also an expression of friendship.

For Reflection and Prayer

- In what ways is the centurion a role model for you?
- Who needs you to intercede for them? Who needs you to go to Jesus for them?
- If a friend asked to intercede for you, what would you tell her or him you need right now?

Jesus, You know the areas in my life that need healing, but You also know the sicknesses—physical, spiritual, and emotional—in the lives of my friends and family. Prompt me to intercede for them and pray for their healing. I trust You to work all things together for their good and Your glory because You are a God who works everything for our good. Amen.

DAY 7
Risky Business

Ten Lepers

O—T TAKE RISKS

As he entered a village there, ten men with leprosy stood at a distance, crying out, "Jesus, Master, have mercy on us!"
                                                            Luke 17:12-13

Read Luke 17:11-19.

As a child, I thought the phrase used for ostracizing people was "treating them like a leopard" instead of the correct one, "treating them like a leper," so the saying made no sense to me because leopards are cool. I have always loved leopard-print stuff; my mom still has my pink leopard pants I wore in high school when I thought I was cool. She threatens to pull them out and show them to the world if I ever get "too big for my britches" (in other words, prideful, for those who don't speak Southern), thinking I am "too cool."

Leprosy, on the other hand, is not cool. According to the Centers for Disease Control and Prevention, it is "an infection caused by slow-growing bacteria....With early diagnosis and treatment, the disease can be cured.... However, if left untreated, the nerve damage can result in crippling of hands and feet, paralysis, and blindness."[1]

The law of Moses forbade people with leprosy from remaining in their communities, worshipping in the synagogue or temple, or leading normal lives with their families. This meant disconnection and isolation, the inability to make a living, purposelessness, hopelessness, and a lack of physical touch. Those afflicted with leprosy even had to warn people who came close to them by yelling, "Unclean! Unclean!" so as not to spread the disease (see Numbers 5:1-3 and Deuteronomy 23:14).

When I think about the lepers, I think about the COVID-19 pandemic that began in 2020. In the early days of the pandemic, people hoarded toilet paper, stocked their pantries with canned soup, and made judgmental faces at anyone who sneezed or coughed. As a person who struggles with allergies, I cannot begin to count the number of times that a sneeze from my direction brought about dirty looks, flurries of antibacterial activities, and fear in the faces of those around me. That in no way compares to having leprosy, but the feelings of isolation and judgment were real!

---

1 Centers for Disease Control and Prevention, "Hansen's Disease (Leprosy)," https://www.cdc.gov/leprosy/index.html, accessed December 9, 2020.

When these ten lepers crossed paths with Jesus, they were desperate. (Have you ever been desperate for healing?) They likely had tried every remedy that their culture offered, but to no avail. They asked for help and mercy from Jesus. They humbled themselves in hopes that the rumors about Jesus's ability to heal others were true.

Despite the fact that Luke's account says the lepers were "at a distance," Jesus healed them. Jesus's ability to perform miracles has no boundaries, and He chose to heal from "a distance," knowing that they needed healing.

I am certainly familiar with the pangs of disconnection. Again, not to the extent of a leper, of course, but I have felt left out, isolated, unclean, and disregarded. I have felt "less than" by being too much on numerous occasions: too fat, too tall, too smart, too loud, too enthusiastic, too religious, too much. I have my fair share of scars from the labels others placed on me, but I am also aware that I may have, in my own insecurity, inflicted scars on others.

> **Jesus risked the scrutiny of others because He chose to love all people.**

Jesus chose to put Himself in contact with the outcasts of his day—

the castoffs of society—like the lepers in this story. He also hung out with tax collectors (another group of outcasts) and "sinners" (Luke 5:30 NIV). Jesus risked the scrutiny of others because He chose to love *all* people, not just those who looked good and acted properly—and it ultimately led Him to the cross.

Loving others is risky business. The question is, What are *you* willing to risk to develop friendships with others?

For Reflection and Prayer

- Has someone ever taken a risk in reaching out to you? What happened?
- What can you do when you feel disconnected from other people?
- Whom do you want to know on a deeper level? Are you willing to take the risk?

Lord, thank You for being willing to meet people where they are. Thank You for those who have taken risks to love me. Help me do the same. Give me the courage to take risks in order to develop deeper, closer relationships with others. Amen.

DAY 8
Well, Well, Well

The Woman at the Well

Jesus replied, "If you only knew the gift God has for you and who you are speaking to, you would ask me, and I would give you living water."

John 4:10

Read John 4:1-26, 39-42.

Years ago, my family and I were at a graduation party to celebrate a young man in our life. When we arrived, the house was filled with grandparents, aunts, uncles, and cousins from out of town, other graduates, and a few other guests.

A woman at the party looked so familiar that I could not concentrate on anything else. I racked my brain for places I might have encountered her. And then I asked her.

"Do I know you from somewhere?"

"I don't think so," she responded. "We don't live around here."

"Huh. I know it will come to me eventually." We exchanged awkward smiles and I returned to my family. Later in the evening, I overheard some of the graduates quoting a popular television show. One line was from a character I really love, and once it was spoken, I said, loudly, "I love that show!" My husband glared at me. Was I too loud? Was the show inappropriate in his eyes? I whispered, "What?"

He said (motioning to the lady I had spoken to earlier), "She is on that show!"

Oh. My. Horsefly.

I knew I recognized her. But then I felt foolish. She is a big star in Hollywood and I am a teacher at a private school in a dusty city. She is glamorous and I rarely wear lip color. She has an agent and I have . . . well, a loud mouth. What did we possibly have in common? I will tell you: We both wanted to celebrate this young graduate. I was his favorite teacher and she is his favorite aunt. We had something in common.

Jesus and the Samaritan woman came from different cultures, were different genders, and worshipped differently; but they found something in common. Jesus used the topic of water as a bridge into a deeper conversation. Even though the woman asked all sorts of questions and brought up all sorts of topics, Jesus was determined to connect with her on a deeper level—at the point of her greatest need.

> **Finding common ground you share with another is a beginning point of connection.**

At various events I have participated in an interpersonal bingo game of sorts. In order to clear a space, one has to find someone who shares something in common—What is your favorite food? In what state were you born? Are you right-handed or left-handed? What show have you binged on Netflix? It is always eye-opening to identify people who share interests, issues, and idiosyncrasies. It helps me feel more connected, even to folks I do not know well. Such commonalities, albeit a bit superficial, foster connection—and, often, a lot of fun!

As you build relationships with others, connection is key. Finding common ground you share with another is a beginning point of connection. It can be a hobby, a favorite TV show, or even a common love for God. Those places and spaces can become bridges into deeper conversations and shared experiences that enrich both of your lives.

For Reflection and Prayer

- Think about a friendship you enjoy. How did you make connections?

- Think about a person you'd like to know. What common ground might you share? How could you use those connection points?
- Think of someone from a different culture or religious background from yours. How can you build a bridge to that person?

Lord, thank You for pursuing me and meeting my deepest needs. You created me for a relationship with You and for relationships with others. Help me to find bridges and connections with other people, and allow those friendships to reflect Your unconditional love, forgiveness, and grace. Amen.

DAY 9

Hanging Out by the Pool

The Sick Man at the Pool

O━┳ PURSUE WELLNESS

Jesus told him, "Stand up, pick up your mat, and walk!"

Instantly, the man was healed! He rolled up his sleeping mat and began walking!

John 5:8-9a

Read John 5:1-9a.

I had strep throat a couple times as a kid. I got mono in fifth grade. (Although it is called the "kissing disease," I caught it under much less romantic circumstances—a water fountain!) But I have never been really sick, praise the Lord.

Hanging Out by the Pool

I have broken a few toes, but despite lots of sports activities, a few car accidents, occasional clumsiness, outdoor adventures, and teenage shenanigans, I have never been seriously injured.

However, I do struggle with a malady—an obsession with food. For decades, I have cooked it, planned it, thought about it, shopped for it, enjoyed it, fed others with it, watched a bazillion television shows about it (Who can name all the Food Network chefs and judges? Me!), dreamed about it, overconsumed it, and cursed it when I stepped on the scale.

I have also struggled with my weight for most of my life— an outward consequence for an inward imbalance. But I rarely speak about it because it embarrasses me. It mortifies me. But one day, I sat down with a trusted friend and spilled my guts. I told her all my struggles with food, my envy of those who seem to consume food for fuel only, my desire to have self-control and honor God with my health, and my shame at making food an idol. It felt so good to share these burdens with a safe person and receive prayer.

When we meet the man at the pool of Bethesda, he was not having a good day. He was working on four decades of bad days. The man had been sitting at the edge of a pool for thirty-eight years, on his mat, waiting to be healed from his sufferings as an invalid. I actually hate that term *invalid*. No one should be made to feel less than, and certainly not invalid—not valid.

But there he was, surrounded by others who were also on the struggle bus of sickness—the blind, the lame, the paralyzed. They were all waiting for an angel of the Lord to stir the waters

37

in hopes that they would be the first one into the pool to receive healing.

When Jesus approached the man, his first act was to ask the man a question: "Would you like to get well?" (v. 6). What kind of question is that, Jesus? Of course he wanted to get well, right?

Actually, the man responded with an excuse. He told Jesus that he had no one to help him get closer to the healing pool, so he missed his chance for healing each time. What he did not know was that he was talking with the Great Physician. He didn't see the One in front of him who could truly help because he was living in a world of excuses, resentment, and disappointment. After all that time, had he given up? I probably would have.

One time, I was on a return flight to Phoenix. When we landed almost twenty minutes early, everyone on the plane recognized that something was not right. The ground crew was acting strange. All of us immediately got on our phones to discover that there was a bomb scare at the airport into which we were flying. Someone in the drop-off portion of the airport had abandoned a car, and the airport security dogs alerted their officers that there might be an explosive in the trunk. To ensure our safety, we sat at the gate for over two hours. People were grumpy, impatient, hungry, and afraid.

After the first hour, one of the passengers pulled out her suitcase in which she had enough snacks for everyone on the plane. The employees allowed her the chance to get on the plane loudspeaker and share her story. She admitted that she had been stuck on a flight for another reason at one time and had promised herself she would never feel so trapped on a plane again. She was offering each passenger the opportunity to have a snack because on a previous flight she too had felt grumpy, impatient, hungry, and afraid. An unpleasant experience from her past helped her encourage others in the present.

> **We all have something in our lives... that is keeping us from being well or whole.**

When we are willing to share our experiences (and even our snacks) with others, friendships with Jesus and others can deepen. Even though it may not be paralysis or food or excuses, we all have something in our lives—sometimes more than one thing—that is keeping us from being well or whole. And like the lame man, Jesus is willing to heal us, but we may be so used to our situation that we miss what Jesus is offering. If we want wholeness—whether in relationships or our physical bodies— we need to surrender our lives to the One who can make us well.

For Reflection and Prayer

- In what area of your life do you need healing from God? Do you want to get well? Why or why not?

- How has God brought wholeness and healing to you in the past? Thank Him for it.
- Is there an area in your life you've been dealing with so long that you don't think change could ever happen? Tell God about it now.

Lord, I admit that sometimes I get so stuck in my thinking and behavior patterns that I lose faith in Your ability to bring healing and wholeness. I do believe! Help my unbelief. Lord, You know my heart—help me become a person who pursues wholeness in You. Give me the strength to let go of my selfish desires, my disappointments, and my resentment. I need Your healing, Lord. Amen.

DAY 10
A Little Help from My Friends

The Paralyzed Man on the Mat

O━┳ ACCEPT HELP

Seeing their faith, Jesus said to the man, "Young man, your
sins are forgiven."

Luke 5:20

Read Luke 5:17-26.

I hate asking for help. I would rather have a bikini wax than call someone and ask for assistance. Call it pride, call it stubbornness, call it stupidity—all those things are probably true—but it is a problem for me, nonetheless. I really love helping others, but when the tables are turned, it makes me uncomfortable.

It takes humility to accept help from another person. But it also allows someone else the blessings of being selfless, serving, giving, and being the hands and feet of Jesus.

I have a friend who once came upon an injured dog on a busy street. Although the dog did not belong to her, she tried to get it to safety and get it medical help, but the dog refused. His bark and growls discouraged her from picking him up. She finally called animal control for instructions and waited for them to arrive.

Sometimes, I am afraid that my own insecurities, brokenness, and emotional injuries stop me from asking for help. I am much like that injured pooch, unable to see kindness and a desire to help for what they are—the love of God demonstrated through another person.

The paralyzed man in Luke 5 had some incredible friends. Maybe he asked for help or maybe they just took the initiative, but either way, the man had a plan and a clan. His "mat mates" were committed to getting this man to Jesus so he could be healed!

The friends were strong. They carried this grown man on a mat to see Jesus.

They were tenacious. When they could get close enough (this was way before handicapped parking), they made a hole in the roof of a house to lower the man down.

They were bold. They placed him right in front of Jesus, in the middle of the crowd, with expectation and without apology. They demonstrated great faith.

42

But the paralyzed man demonstrated an important character trait, too. He was willing to accept help. He was humble enough to admit his need and smart enough to know he couldn't meet that need on his own.

Our son, Josiah, is sixteen years old and six feet four inches tall. If he had a nickel for every time I have asked him to reach a top shelf for a dish, he could afford a pair of shoes for his size fourteen feet. When I am in the kitchen and call his name, he often enters and just asks, "Which dish do you need?" He already knows there is something that is literally above my abilities. I think it reminds him that he is loved and trusted, and it reminds me that I cannot do all things alone.

I wonder if the Beatles wrote the song "Help" to encourage those of us who hesitate to ask others for assistance. Asking for help takes self-awareness and humility. It takes trust in God and the other person.

> **Accepting help is not weakness; it reveals the strength of humility.**

The paralyzed man knew he needed help. He knew he had friends willing to assist him. He trusted them to place him before Jesus, knowing he could not seek Him on his own.

Our own weaknesses can pave the way for us to recognize the areas in which we need to grow and the people around us who might help. Such weaknesses can be the open door to friendship and vulnerability. This is a lesson we all can learn from the paralyzed man. Accepting help is not weakness; it reveals the strength of humility.

For Reflection and Prayer

- What is your typical response when someone offers to help you?
- Whom do you turn to when you need help?
- How can accepting help deepen your relationships?

God, thank You for putting people in my life who are willing to help me when I need it. Give me the humility to ask for help instead of being prideful. Forgive me for trying to do life on my own without You. And Father, please give me the discernment to know when I need to help others. Amen.

DAY 11
Cross Connections

The Dying Thief

⚿ OFFER GRACE AND FORGIVENESS

Then he said, "Jesus, remember me when you come into your Kingdom."

And Jesus replied, "'I assure you, today you will be with me in paradise."

Luke 23:42-43

Read Luke 23:32, 39-43.

My family loves watching war movies. I spend most of the time peering through my fingers as the shots fly and the blood spills, but there is something so powerful about watching history unfold on the big screen (or a smaller screen at home). I often do at least one ugly cry before the movie ends. I am a big chicken, but I am also a sucker for a compelling story. These movies are often filled with beautiful, imperfect people triumphing over harrowing circumstances.

45

> **When we admit our need for redemption in Jesus, we receive mercy and grace.**

On the day Jesus went to the cross, the ultimate battle—the fight for our souls—was underway in the spiritual realm. It was a fight for our redemption and release from sin's captivity, and it took place on the battlefield in Golgotha. The story starred the Son of God but involved two other characters, the thieves who were crucified and placed on either side of Jesus.

One mocked Him but the other did not. One remained unrepentant but the other recognized who Jesus was and sought forgiveness. Both men died alongside Jesus, but only one saw Jesus in paradise. Jesus forgave the man who surrendered to Him in the last hours of his life.

This man's redemption is symbolic of all of humanity. When we admit our need for redemption in Jesus, we receive mercy and grace. He forgives us and restores us to right relationship with the Father.

When I think of unearned grace, I remember the story of some acquaintances of ours who had an experience of grace at Disneyland they will never forget. Disneyland had launched an anniversary campaign in which they were giving away a car every day during the campaign. We were living in Southern California at the time and had annual passes to the Magic Kingdom. So, we had tried to win the car numerous times without success.

In order to have a chance to win the car, you needed a special ticket to place into a large slot machine of sorts. It was exciting to put in a ticket and pull the handle, even when the chances were slim to none that you would win the car and take it home.

These folks had spent a long day at Disneyland, and their daughter came across one of the tickets on the ground. They had already tried to win the car earlier in the day to no avail. They attempted to take the ticket to a cast member, but the employee told them that there was no way to track the tickets, and that they were free to try their luck again. The cast member encouraged them by saying that no one had won the car that day, and with only an hour or so left in the day, it might be a good time to try. And try they did! Their daughter put the ticket in the slot machine, pulled the arm, and then squealed when the machine's lights flashed.

They had won a car with a ticket that they had not earned. They drove home in a new car with profound gratitude. In the years to follow, they always graciously provided rides home from youth group and school for students who needed it because they were well aware they had been given a gift that day and needed to act in such a way as to reflect their gratitude.

The thief on the cross who recognized Jesus's innocence was promised that he would be with Jesus in heaven. A man who did not deserve forgiveness was given grace in the present and a promise of a hopeful future.

Jesus extended grace and forgiveness to this man, giving us an example to follow. He extends that same grace and forgiveness to each of us, and because of that, we can give the same to others. We have the chance every day in every relationship to act in such a way as to reflect the gratitude we have for the sacrifice of Jesus on the cross.

For Reflection and Prayer

- Look back at how Jesus treated the men crucified on either side of Him. Which of Jesus's traits or actions can you apply in your relationships right now?
- In your life, who needs to hear about God's grace and forgiveness? Whom do you need to forgive and offer grace?
- Besides Jesus, who has shown you grace and offered you forgiveness when you needed it most?

Lord, thank You for sending Jesus to die for the sins of the world. Thank You, Jesus, for setting an example of how to treat others, despite fatigue and unimaginable pain. Help me to treat others with grace and mercy, even when I am treated unfairly. Give me love for others and help me to forgive when I'm tempted to harbor resentment or disappointment. Amen.

DAY 12
Rise and Shine

The Widow of Nain's Son

O━╤ SHOW COMPASSION

When the Lord saw her, his heart overflowed with compassion. "Don't cry!" he said.

Luke 7:13

Read Luke 7:11-17.

As far as I know, the first death I experienced was that of Bambi's mom. You probably remember that classic Disney movie. Although the audience did not see the death occur, the sound of the gunshot in the forest is forever etched in my mind.

Then, I watched the movie *Old Yeller*. After reading the book, my fifth-grade class went to see the movie. I had read the book and I knew the ending, but when the house lights came up, I had lost all my tears and nasal mucus over a faithful dog. (As an aside, a student in my class had thrown a wad of chewed bubble gum and it landed inside my mane of curly locks. I told everyone that was the reason my face was so tear-stained.)

However, nothing quite prepared me for *The Lion King*. Disney knows how to pull on all my heartstrings, and this story was no exception. My dad had passed away shortly before the movie was released, so when the story began to unfold, I connected to the story of a young lion cub, Simba, and his loving father, Mufasa, who was voiced by the great James Earl Jones. (That man could read the ingredients to a box of crackers and I would pass the offering plate.)

The relationship between the two was cut short when Simba's evil uncle killed the great Mufasa. Even before the death occurred, I could see tragedy approaching, and the tears began to well up in my eyes. When the great Lion King fell to his death, I soaked our bucket of popcorn with tears and covered my mouth to muffle my sobs. I kept reminding myself that it was an animated film and that I was probably scaring the little kids in my vicinity. I assured myself with the fact that James Earl Jones was very much alive, but then I remembered that my dad was not. I continued to cry long after the attendants began cleaning the theater when the movie was over.

In Luke 7, Jesus had just healed the centurion's servant (vv. 1-10). He was headed into the next city when He saw a funeral procession of sorts. He also saw a grieving mother (who was a widow) as she mourned her only son.

Jesus took the time to stop and show compassion to a brokenhearted woman. Before He encouraged her to stop crying and before He healed her son, verse 13 says, "The Lord saw her." Jesus stopped and acknowledged this woman's plight and pain. He had compassion for her. Jesus is never too busy to see a need and show compassion.

Jesus took the time to touch the bier (casket and its holder) and He commanded the son to rise. From the story of the centurion earlier in the chapter, we know Jesus could have healed from a distance and without touching anyone or anything. Yet, Jesus stopped and gave His full attention to a widow in her deepest anguish. He resurrected a boy that day, but He also restored a family and revived hope, too.

In the parable about connection at the beginning of this book, in which I share about my birthday hiking trip in the Grand Canyon, I failed to mention one person: my sister. My amazing sister, Allyson, wanted to celebrate my fiftieth birthday with me, and so she flew with her sons to Phoenix.

Sadly, when they arrived in Phoenix late in the evening, she realized that she had left her driver's license somewhere in the airport in Houston. The lack of ID disallowed her from picking up the vehicle she had already reserved and prepaid. She was 230 miles from her destination without anyone to come and get her. My family and I were already at the Grand Canyon, preparing for a very early morning start the next day, and it was already after 8:00 p.m.

Allyson flagged down an Uber driver and explained the situation. She was tired, frustrated, and disappointed, but she was also determined. The driver told her that he did not have enough money to buy the gas needed to get them to their destination, but she assured him that although she was without a license, she had a debit card and would take care of the gas and anything else necessary to transport the three of them to the canyon. After a long drive and a very expensive Uber trip, they safely arrived.

I cannot express how special it made me feel to have them come all that way, sacrifice so much, and take the journey down into the Grand Canyon with me. But that is what friendship—including friendship with a sister—takes sometimes. Friendship takes a willingness to go out of our way for another, to compassionately sacrifice time and energy and walk alongside another on his or her journey, no matter the cost.

Jesus modeled compassion in His interactions with the widow and her son. If we want our friendships to thrive, we need to follow the example He set. We need to give full attention to the other person and, when appropriate, offer assistance. To do

> **Friendship takes a willingness to go out of our way for another... no matter the cost.**

so validates the other person's needs and feelings so that trust between us can develop. Shared experiences of compassion like this are the building blocks of friendship.

For Reflection and Prayer

- Who in your life makes you feel known and understood? What do they do to communicate this?
- What keeps you from giving others your undivided attention?
- How do you like to demonstrate compassion? Who needs you to show compassion to them?

God, even in my busyness, please give me eyes to see those who are hurting. Please help me slow down long enough to show compassion for the pain of others and take the time to help in any way I can. Amen.

DAY 13
The Eyes Have It

The Blind Man

O—⚷ SHOW BOLDNESS

And Jesus said, "All right, receive your sight! Your faith has healed you."

Luke 18:42

Read Luke 18:35-43.

I have a hard time asking for what I want. Even with my own kids, I will say, "When you have a moment, I could use some help in the kitchen." Oftentimes, I have completed the task before they arrive, and then I am not happy. I never say, "I need your help right now," even when that is exactly what I need.

When my son is playing video games, I say, "When you get to a stopping place, dinner is almost ready." He is sixteen years old and loves video games, so until Jesus comes back, finding a stopping place is impossible. I never say, "Time's up; dinner is ready." Actually, I do say it, but only when I have waited and waited for him to disengage and have lost my patience and my temper.

I do not like this about myself. I admire people who are confident enough to state what they need. The friends in my life who approach our friendship like this are so refreshing. They articulate clearly what they need, and I can choose to meet those needs—or not. But there is no questioning. On the other hand, I am the princess of ambiguity.

The blind man at the gates of Jericho did not struggle with ambiguity; he was bold and forthright. He was begging for money and food from travelers and passersby when Jesus and His posse walked past. The blind man could hear the crowd walking by and asked why there was such a fervor. Someone explained to him that Jesus of Nazareth was in the crowd.

At that point, the blind man showed the boldness of someone who was desperate for help. He cried out, "Son of David, have mercy on me!" (v. 39). The term "Son of David" referred to a prophecy that the Messiah would come from the lineage of David (2 Samuel 7:12-13). In calling Jesus the Son of David, the blind man was declaring Jesus as the Messiah—a bold claim few would make and a huge risk few would take.

Despite the rebuke of the crowd, he continued his bold pursuit of Jesus. He raised the stakes even higher by shouting even more, and his boldness did not go unnoticed.

> **Being bold with a heart like Jesus will make [healthy] connections more possible and more beautiful.**

Jesus stopped and asked for the blind man to be brought to Him. When the two met, Jesus did not make small talk. Straight away, He asked the man to state what he wanted. Jesus understood this man's candor, so He responded in kind. The blind man boldly proclaimed, "Lord... I want to see!" (v. 41). And when the blind man received his sight, he was bold in his praise to God.

I cannot relate to this type of boldness, but I appreciate those who can speak this way. I realize how much richer and deeper my relationships would be if I stated directly and clearly what I need (and want) and what I think. When I call a friend for insight and she is too busy to take my call, I wish I had the boldness to say in a voice mail message or text, "Please call. I need prayerful advice." When a person tries to give me advice instead of just listening, I wish I had the boldness to say, "Thank you, but what I really need is some empathy." When I receive a phone call and the person on the other end is the one who needs support, I wish I consistently set an example of vulnerability, making the phone call easier.

I certainly want to have boldness like this blind man, but even more, I want to have a heart like Jesus. A heart that makes time for others, even when it goes against my schedule. A heart that can be interrupted when another is hurting. A heart that asks what the other person wants instead of doing what I think is best. A heart that sees faith in others and encourages them. If we are going to foster healthy relationships in our connections with others, being bold with a heart like Jesus will make such connections more possible and more beautiful.

For Reflection and Prayer

- How would your friendships be different if you were to clearly state what you want and think?
- How would your relationship with God be different if you were to demonstrate the same boldness as the blind man?
- Do you become defensive around people who are candid and direct? Why or why not?

Father, thank You that I can approach Your throne with confidence because of Jesus. Give me courage to be bold in my relationships with others, and give me bold faith to show others Your love. Amen.

DAY 14
Straighten Up

The Crippled Woman

O—┳ BE REAL

When Jesus saw her, he called her over and said, "Dear woman, you are healed of your sickness!"

Luke 13:12

Read Luke 13:10-17.

A few winters back, my family traveled to Texas to visit my side of the family.

My sister had the brilliant idea for the entire family to get pictures taken together while we were all there. She hired a fantastic photographer, we all got dolled up, and we headed to the studio. But this particular photographer specializes in outdoor photography.

Did I mention it was winter?

We got individual photos. Photos with the cousins. Snapshots with sisters. Most of all, what we got was cold. The longer the photo shoot lasted, the colder it got. When it was over, we thanked the photographer and had a bonding experience with the heaters in our cars.

Weeks later, we got the proofs from the photographer. The pictures were amazing. She had done an extraordinary job capturing each person—and no one looked cold. No one. We had all put on our smiles and ignored our discomfort long enough to take the pictures. No one would guess that we were all freezing our patooties off. We did a good job hiding it.

The crippled woman in Luke 13 could not hide her discomfort. She had been "crippled by an evil spirit...for eighteen years" (v. 11) and could not stand up straight. Her issue was both spiritual and physical in nature. She could not hide behind a smile. For eighteen years, she had suffered. She had watched the stares of religious leaders who believed physical ailments were a sign of sin. For almost two decades, she saw the feet of people instead of their faces, the ground instead of the sky.

Then Jesus saw her. He interrupted His teaching and called her forward. He laid His hands on her and healed her. The passage does not explain how a spirit could affect a person so negatively (especially one who was faithful enough to the synagogue), but we know that her immediate responses were gratitude and worship.

I love that Jesus did not ask this woman to be healed before she came to Him. She came before Him hunched over and broken. She did not try and "straighten up" before she stood before Jesus. She came just as she was. Sometimes, I think I need to have my "poop in a group" before I go to Him with my issues, concerns, and hurts.

I wish we had before-and-after photos of this woman. Her story is a testament to the power of God and His care for His people. Her story is also a reminder of what it looks like to be real before God and others.

In today's culture, with Instagram filters and the ability to crop out the parts of pictures we don't like, we get an inaccurate picture of the lives of others. Social media has encouraged us to post "highlights" of our daily lives, but the truth is, life is not all highlights. In fact, there are lots of lowlights (and medium lights) in life, yet we "straighten up" our lives before we post. But God is not interested in only our highlights; He cares about every detail, every heartache, every celebration, every off day, every triumph, every care, and everything that

> **God is not interested in only our highlights; He cares about every detail, every heartache.**

crosses our personal radar. And He does not want us to sugar-coat it, hide it, filter it, put lipstick on it, or suppress it. He wants us, just like the crippled woman, to go before Him and be healed.

For Reflection and Prayer

- In what area of your life do you wish Jesus would say, "Woman, you are set free from your infirmity"? Is there a physical, emotional, or spiritual issue that is crippling you in some way?
- What are you like in front of others? Are you real and transparent, or do you try to hide your struggles and wounds?
- With whom can you be yourself? What might happen if you dropped your guard to allow others to see who you really are?

Father, thank You for being a God of love and of healing. Please help me to discern when people are hurting, even when they hide behind a smile. Let my kindness be a healing balm in their lives; please use me to encourage others for Your glory. Father, give me the assurance and courage to come before You in weakness and vulnerability; in Jesus's name. Amen.

DAY 15
Naked Truth

The Demon-possessed Man

O—т EXPERIENCE CHANGE

"Go back to your family, and tell them everything God has done for you."

Luke 8:39a

Read Luke 8:27–39.

Recently, a friend of mine who owns a farm was shocked to find a stranger on her property. She was feeding her animals early one morning when she heard a voice and turned around to find a completely nude woman standing in the middle of her field. The nudist had wandered from a retreat center a few miles away wearing nothing but tattoos and somehow ended up on my friend's farm. My friend pointed her in the direction of the main street to get back to the retreat center and then went back to her farming. But the experience was shocking and won't be forgotten!

The account of the demon-possessed man in Luke 8 was shocking as well. Sometimes, Bible stories are so sensible and tame, but this one is downright spectacular! It has all the components of a *Game of Thrones* episode: nudity, battle, death, and livestock.

Jesus had crossed the lake from Galilee and upon getting out of the boat, He was approached by a man—demon-possessed, homeless, desperate, isolated, and nude. Verse 29 (NIV) tells us that the man "had broken his chains and had been driven by the demon into solitary places." (Oftentimes, isolation exacerbates whatever else we are dealing with.) The man slept in the tombs and had no real hope for the future.

What a scene to behold! Jesus went right to work. When He began to command the legion of demons out of this man, they recognized immediately who He was— "Jesus, Son of the Most High God" (v. 28 NIV). The disciples may not have been certain of the identity of Jesus, but these demons knew they were battling against the Lord of Hosts.

The demons begged Jesus to send them into nearby livestock. He gave them permission to leave the man and go into a nearby herd of pigs. The pigs then rushed over a cliff and drowned themselves—a waste of perfectly good bacon, but a perfect way to dispel demons.

Those tending the pigs ran off to tell others what had happened (this stuff isn't covered in pig-herding school). By the time they returned with others from the town, the man was sane, dressed, and sitting at the feet of Jesus. What a contrast. From nude, insane, and isolated to dressed, sane, and hanging out with Jesus. The eyewitnesses recounted the story and instead of feeling excitement and awe, the townspeople were afraid. They sent Jesus away from their town out of fear.

The man was not afraid of Jesus—he begged to go with Him. However, Jesus instructed the man to return home and tell everyone what God had done for him. Verse 39b (NIV) says the man "went away and told all over town how much Jesus had done for him."

When someone in my life loses a lot of weight, goes on a fantastic vacation, falls in love, has a baby, gets a new job, or wins a competition, he or she is often quick to let the world know. When America watched Tom Cruise jump on Oprah's couch years ago, we knew something wonderful had happened in his life. He had fallen in love! If the demon-possessed man had been given the chance to jump on a talk show legend's couch in excitement when he was freed, I think he might have. His healing was the best thing that could have happened to him. He received freedom from the demons, covering from his nakedness and shame, and the chance to rediscover community once again.

The man whom Jesus met that day was naked, possessed, and afraid—but once Jesus healed him, he was free, truly free. And he was glad to tell everyone what God had done for him.

When we encounter Jesus in a powerful way, everything changes. For God's glory and with His help, we too can be freed like this man—from shame, from disconnection, and from isolation. We can walk in freedom and tell everyone we meet about how great our God is.

> **We can walk in freedom and tell everyone we meet about how great our God is.**

For Reflection and Prayer

- In what ways can you relate to this man?
- How does this story give you hope?
- Do you know someone who needs the hope that this story offers?
- How can you share with others how Jesus has changed you and your life?

God, thank You for setting me free. Thank You for seeing past my brokenness and shame and making a way for me to live in freedom. Thank You for clothing me with dignity and strength. Help me to remember and to share how You've changed me, especially when I encounter others who are caught in the prisons that sin creates. Amen.

DAY 16

The Company You Keep

Tax Collectors

As Jesus was walking along, he saw a man named Matthew sitting at his tax collector's booth. "Follow me an be my disciple," Jesus said to him. So Matthew got up and followed him.

Matthew 9:9

Read Matthew 9:9-13.

I am always intrigued with celebrities. I know I shouldn't be—they are just people, faulty and human like me. Although I do not care for all the gossip that often goes with celebrity, I love happy stories that involve the folks I admire on the screen, big and small. On more than one occasion, when meeting a celebrity, I lose all ability to speak intelligible English. It is painful.

One of my favorite celebrity stories is of funnyman Conan O'Brien. This goofy, awkward, and often hilarious talk show host has had a long career of making others laugh. But he also tells a sweet story of how he met his wife.[1]

To make a long story short, she was in the audience of a taping of a show Conan was on. He fell for a fan. It was a Cinderella story of sorts—the common girl finds a celebrity prince and they run off into the paparazzi sunset together.

Similarly, Matt Damon met his beautiful bride in a bar while she was working. He had already gained some celebrity and hid behind the bar to get away from all the drunk fans. She put him to work and they married soon after.[2]

Contrasts make for great stories.

When Jesus first met Matthew, it was a contrast extravaganza! Matthew was a tax collector; they were the bad guys of that day. They collected taxes and often skimmed a percentage for themselves. They were hated by the public and despised by the poor.

But Matthew's occupation did not discourage Jesus. In contrast to society, He saw beyond the position, the checkered history, and the opinion of others and called the tax collector to

---

1 Kate Marin, "What We Know about Conan O'Brien's Wife, Liza Powel," The Netline, April 8, 2020, https://thenetline.com/the-untold-truth-of-conan-obrien-wife/, accessed December 10, 2020.

2 Sophie Tedmanson, "The Real, Never-before-heard Story of How Matt and Lucy Damon Met," Vogue, May 16, 2018, https://www.vogue.com.au/celebrity/news /the-real-never-before-heard-story-of-how-matt-and-lucy-damon-met/news -story/823ebcc12e68ecc1f6f836db633599e6, accessed December 10, 2020.

follow Him. Jesus and His disciples even joined Matthew and his posse of sinners for dinner.

This was scandalous in the eyes of the Pharisees. The contrast was too great for their religious minds to accept. They spent their lives avoiding sinful people like germaphobes avoid germs. Jesus could not possibly come from God, or else He would know better than to rub elbows with the likes of Matthew.

In contrast to the religious leaders, Jesus saw the potential of Matthew. He pulled Matthew from his tax-collecting booth and his life of deception and gave him the opportunity to find a life of meaning and purpose. Jesus called out the best in Matthew, took the time to disciple him, and gave him the mission of proclaiming the kingdom of God.

Jesus does indeed see potential in people. After all, He made us and knows what we can do—even if we ourselves do not see it.

Jesus saw the potential of Simon Peter to be a rock (John 1:42).

Jesus saw the potential of Saul, also known as Paul, to be an apostle (Acts 9:1-12).

Jesus saw the potential of fishermen brothers to be fishers of men (Matthew 4:19).

Jesus also sees the potential in us, and He calls us to see it in other people—to speak life into them and help them see just how amazing God has created them. He can give us eyes to see the beauty and struggle of others and the potential of how God can use those things to point others to Him.

True friends have the potential to see the best in us. They encourage us to pursue God's calling. They see in us what we may not see in ourselves, and they bring those traits to life by naming them and challenging us to develop them. Most of all, they celebrate when they see us becoming all God wants us to be.

True friends have the potential to see the best in us.

For Reflection and Prayer

- Who sees the potential in you and encourages you to pursue God's best for you?
- In your sphere of influence, who needs to know their potential instead of their past? Who might not see the potential in themselves?
- Thank God for the contrast in your life since you became a Christian.

Lord, thank You for making a way to bridge the contrast between You and Your people. Thank You for Jesus, who died on the cross to remove the barrier and foster connection. Make me like You, Lord. Help me see the potential in others, not just their faults and flaws. Help me love others the way Jesus did. Amen.

DAY 17
Blind Faith

Saul

As he was approaching Damascus on this mission, a light from heaven suddenly shone down around him.

Acts 9:3

Read Acts 9:1-22.

When I was in high school, there was a really cute boy on the football team. (I wish so many of my stories did not start with, "There was a boy," but here we are.) He did not seem to notice me, but I certainly noticed him.

One day, when I was walking home from soccer practice, it started to rain, really rain. Arizona is known for its dry climate, so when it rains, the skies open and the ground cannot keep up with the precipitation. The streets had begun to flood. I was not

worried about getting wet; the air was still warm and my hair—
the same curly mane I have donned all my life—Is not afraid of
water either. It felt good after a long soccer practice.

I was about a mile from home when, out of the corner of
my eye, I saw his vehicle. The football player's car was distinct,
so I knew it was him. I did my best to walk without tripping and
tried to look as cool as a soaking-wet sophomore possibly can. I
was on the opposite side of the street from the lane he would be
driving on, but my heart raced as his car got closer. I could hear
his car radio getting louder as he got closer to me. I did not dare
turn around; I just wanted to focus on not embarrassing myself
with clumsiness. The streets were deluged with rain by this
point, especially the gutters, and I did not want to accidentally
step into one.

He had his window rolled down and just before he reached
me, I could hear that his car was filled with other football players—who were laughing. What I did not know at the time was
that they were laughing at me. The driver saw a huge collection
of water in the gutter—an opportunity to cover an unsuspecting
pedestrian (me) with a wall of water—so he crossed to my side
of the road and did just that.

The wave of gutter water must have been eight feet high. It
was heavy when it landed on me, soaking every fiber of my body,
including my pride. The only thing worse was the laughter that
came from the car. They were laughing at me. Heartily.

71

My crush on that boy turned quickly into a desire to crush his face. My anger and mortification quickly turned into a desire for revenge. A nearby stone became my weapon of choice. Years of softball pitching served me well. I chucked that stone at the back of the car, and the sound of rain was overshadowed by the crash of the back window of the car. There was no laughter coming from the car anymore.

Reality kicked in and I ran. I turned and found the closest place to hide, and when I knew it was safe, I ran home. My heart stopped racing sometime that evening. The next day at school, I avoided eye contact with everyone on the football team, even the water boy.

My one and only encounter with this boy was on that road and it changed things forever.

The apostle Paul was not always the letter writer, powerful leader, and proponent of Jesus. Prior to his conversion, he oversaw the death of Christians, sought to destroy the early church, and threatened the disciples. Then one day Paul, also known as Saul, was walking on the road to Damascus when he encountered Jesus.

Despite all the harm that Paul had done, Jesus had a plan for his life. Paul became one of the first missionaries/church planters/Christian authors in the first century. He penned over 25 percent of the New Testament,[1] and his letters to the early churches

---

[1] "How Much of the New Testament Was Written by Paul?" December 3, 2020, https://www.alecsatin.com/how-much-of-the-new-testament-was-written-by-paul/, accessed December 10, 2020.

continue to impact the church today.

Often, we encounter God while we are just doing everyday life and work—including those times when we are going our own way and living contrary to God's best for us. It was not unusual for Saul to walk to Damascus, and on this occasion, he was on a mission to persecute Jesus's followers. But God interrupted that common activity in a very uncommon way in order to change Paul's direction and life forever.

> *Our everyday activities and interactions with people... can have eternal impact.*

We should never underestimate the potential of our everyday activities and interactions with people; such interactions can have eternal impact. A conversation in the grocery store or at soccer practice, a text, an affirmation at church, a hug at a funeral, a comment on social media—God can and does use ordinary encounters and conversations to bring about extraordinary blessings, change, healing, and wholeness.

All it requires on your part is the willingness to have the conversation.

For Reflection and Prayer

- This week, what ordinary conversations or encounters have turned into something more significant?
- How has the affirmation or encouragement of others changed your perspective lately?
- How has a recent conversation with God affected you?

Father, allow me to see You in my everyday activities. Allow me to see others who need Your touch as I go about my day. Use me to encourage those around me at the grocery store, in the post office, and even in my home. Amen.

DAY 18
Front Man

John the Baptist

But John tried to talk him out of it. "I am the one who needs to be baptized by you," he said, "so why are you coming to me?"
Matthew 3:14

Read Matthew 3:13-17.

I have the best cousins. Seriously. On both sides of my family. Time with them was always filled with laughter, games, holiday memories, and more laughter. My only female cousin is a beautiful and successful lady whom I might envy if I didn't love her like crazy. My male cousins are good men who love their families well, and I feel blessed to be in their lives. I am envious of people who have a zip code of cousins, but I love the four I have (plus bonus cousins by marriage).

Recently, at speaking engagements of which I was a part, I was surprised by the attendance of my male cousins and their beautiful brides, in addition to tons of other family members. No one laughed more loudly, clapped with more enthusiasm, and poured on more encouragement than my cousins.

John the Baptist was Jesus's relative. Some Bible versions say they were cousins. They were close in age, and I often wonder if they played together as kids. The Bible does not show them together a lot, but then again, we don't know a lot about Jesus's childhood, so it's entirely possible that they spent time together. When they became adults, however, their relationship didn't look like two cousins or two relatives.

In today's Bible passage, Jesus came to John to be baptized, but John was not having it. Not having it at all. He could not fathom baptizing the Lamb of God (John 1:29).

Baptism is a sign of humility—submitting ourselves to the authority and forgiveness of God, recognizing and admitting our inability to save ourselves. It's an outward act that illustrates our inward repentance. Jesus was sinless, so demonstrating repentance was not the goal in His baptism. Instead, the act of humility in Jesus's baptism served as an example to those who were present, to those in their generation, to John the Baptist, and to those who hadn't yet been born—including you and me.

John was a follower of God, but a flawed one nonetheless. The sinless Jesus could have chosen to baptize Himself, but He chose to encourage John and the followers there by allowing them to be part of the process.

Jesus's baptism also gave people (including us) a glimpse into the dynamic relationship among the Trinity—Father, Son, and Holy Spirit acting in concert with one another.

When our son was very young and my husband and I would be in line at Costco, my son was eager to "help" by placing the items on the conveyor belt. The sweet cashier affirmed his efforts by saying, "Wow. You are a good helper; you should work here."

He looked at her with confusion. "I cannot work here. I don't have a name tag." It never occurred to him that he couldn't work at the big box store because he was in kindergarten; he was just well aware of what he lacked.

Humility is an easy word to say, but not an easy concept to practice. Humility is the awareness of what we are lacking and the practice of pointing to God in the process. Jesus lacked nothing, but He lived the practice of pointing others to His father every day.

> **Humility is the awareness of what we are lacking and the practice of pointing to God in the process.**

Jesus set an example of humility everywhere He went—in associating with "tax collectors and sinners"; in choosing a ragtag group of men to be His disciples; in being mocked, beaten, and hung on the cross; and even in dealing with a relative like John the Baptist.

Sometimes, it is difficult to show kindness and humility to the people who know us the best, those who know our backstory and know how to push our buttons. Whether it's a friend we've known for decades or a relative we've known our whole lives, some people bring out the best—and worst—in us. Being humble and gracious in those frustrating moments is not easy, but it is possible. Jesus is both our example and the one who empowers us with His Spirit to imitate His character.

For Reflection and Prayer

- Who brings out both the best and the worst in you? Why?
- Who demonstrates humility on a consistent basis?
- What would happen in your relationships if you chose the path of humility?

Jesus, allow me to follow Your example of humility with everyone I come in contact with. Show me how I might better serve those I love. Show me how to live in humility and confidence at the same time. Amen.

DAY 19
Just Kidding

The Little Children

Then Jesus called for the children and said to the disciples, "Let the children come to me. Don't stop them! For the Kingdom of God belongs to those who are like these children.

Luke 18:16

Read Luke 18:15-17.

In high school, I loved drama class. (It is probably hard to believe this since I am so quiet and demure.) I loved every improv game, every assignment, every role I was asked to portray, and I even loved the teacher.

One day, our teacher asked us what we thought we wanted to be when we grew up. Easy enough question. At the time, my true answer might have been "Van Halen roadie," but I settled for hotel management (my mom's career field at the time).

79

One of the girls in my class stated that she wanted to be a Broadway actress. The drama teacher was in a particularly foul mood that day (maybe he also wanted to be a Van Halen roadie), and her answer elicited a loud laugh from him. He followed that up with a long list of reasons that such an aspiration was foolish and nearly impossible.

Something in me was incensed. A wave of righteous anger welled up in me and I came to the defense of this (now) crying freshman thespian. She was so emotional, she had neither the ability nor the wherewithal for rebuttal. In a raised voice, I told my teacher that only God could tell a person what she can and cannot do. He responded with a note sending me straight to the principal's office for my insubordination.

I cried all the way to the office, which happened to be across the campus. When I finally went before the principal, I was crying so hard that my words were nearly unintelligible. After a few tissues and some deep breaths, I finally relayed the whole story. He asked two students from the class for their side of the story (which corroborated mine) and then had me stay in the office for the remainder of the class period.

When the bell rang, he sent me on to my next class and thanked me for advocating for a peer. I did not have the heart to tell him that I did not think Miss Broadway would make it on the Great White Way (a nickname for the Theater District in New York City), but I was thankful that I was not in trouble for speaking up.

Although we often think of the Holy Spirit as the advocate (John 14:26), Jesus also advocated for people, like the woman caught in adultery, for example. In Luke 18, He had the chance to advocate for some folks who could not advocate for themselves.

Children are often overlooked in our society. They cannot vote, drive a car, or choose whether or not to go to school. Their lack of experience and knowledge disqualifies them from political panels, most talk show interviews, and game shows.

In the first century, children had even fewer rights. Yet, Jesus stood up for them even though they did not have the ability to advocate for Him in return. They had no money to give, no status to bestow, no political power to sway.

> **Being willing to stick your neck out for others shows loyalty... and gives them confidence to run after their dreams.**

I often think about that girl in my drama class. I wonder if she ever made it big in the Big Apple. I also wonder how long it has been since I advocated for anyone like Jesus did.

Jesus stood up for the disenfranchised while He was on earth.

The wounded. The marginalized. You and me. Jesus advocated for the voiceless, the helpless, the clueless—likewise you and me. Romans 5:8 (NIV) reminds us, "But God demonstrates his own love for us in this: While we were still sinners, Christ died for us." He advocated for us and stood in our place, sacrificing Himself on our behalf.

That's a sign of a good friend. Being willing to stick your neck out for others shows loyalty, lets them know you're in their corner, and gives them confidence to run after their dreams. I hope my classmate pursued hers, and I am grateful for friends who cheered me on to pursue mine.

For Reflection and Prayer

- How have your friends been advocates for you? Think of a few examples.
- Write a note to someone who needs to know you're in their corner, cheering them on because you believe in them.
- Spend a few moments thanking Jesus for being your Advocate before the throne of God.

God, thank You for calling me Your child. Help me see others who need You and need someone to advocate for them. Give me the strength and courage to stand up for the lost, the disenfranchised, and the victimized. Amen.

DAY 20
Scent by God

The Woman with the Perfume

O═╍ BE WILLING TO SACRIFICE

"I tell you the truth, wherever the Good News is preached throughout the world, this woman's deed will be remembered and discussed."

Matthew 26:13

Read Matthew 26:6-13.

While some people love flowery scents, I am a sucker for food-scented items. Give me candles, hand soaps, deodorants, and body spray in vanilla creme, waffle cone, cinnamon, coffee, and sugar cookie, and you have made me a happy girl. If the scent name makes you want to lick the packaging, and there is a coupon for it, that is the one for me.

Perfume in biblical times probably did not smell like something from Bath and Body Works, but it also was more rare and valuable than our modern-day colognes. (Well, except for those really expensive perfumes that cost more than a used car.)

When the woman in Matthew 26:6-13 poured perfume on Jesus's head, it was to show Him honor. She wanted to express her deep gratitude and love for Him. And such a demonstration of honor was costly. Very costly. The account in John 12:1-8 tells us the perfume was worth three hundred denarii, and a denarius was a day's wage at that time. Imagine working for ten months (roughly three hundred days) and then giving away every single cent to pour perfume on a preacher's head. That's crazy. Except when it's Jesus you're anointing.

This woman is not even given a name in this story. Matthew did not include her profession, her family, her influence, or her financial status in his description. Neither did the other Gospel writers. But what we do know about her is admirable: she loved much because she'd been forgiven of much. In her mind and heart, no sacrifice was too great for the One who had loved and restored her to a right relationship with God.

Jesus knew her motives and validated this woman's act of worship. He saw her heart and her willingness to sacrifice. He defended her against the criticism of His followers and praised her kindness and affection. He let everyone know that her self-less act would be talked about for thousands of years to follow. (We're talking about it right now!)

This anonymous woman's story is a great example for you and me to follow. Now, I'm not saying you need to put your family's stability on the line by buying a bunch of costly perfume. I'm saying that relationships involve sacrifice. Sometimes it means giving up your time. Other times it means staying up late or getting up early (and believe me, that can be a sacrifice!). And sometimes it means sacrificing financially for a

Showing you care about someone may require sacrifice.

friend. Situations differ, but the principle is the same: showing you care about someone may require sacrifice—and it often does.

To help a friend move, one must sacrifice strength and time. To pray with a person in need, one must sacrifice pride and time. To encourage a friend with the gift of brownies, one must sacrifice time, ingredients, and self-control not to eat them all. To listen to a friend who needs support, one must sacrifice time, patience, and maybe some cell phone minutes. To share Jesus with someone, one must sacrifice prayer, humility, time, and a heart to see them come to faith.

Jesus understood the importance of sacrifice in His relationship with others—His time, His love, and ultimately His life. The woman in this passage sacrificed what she had to display gratitude to Jesus, and we should do likewise.

For Reflection and Prayer

- Who has sacrificed their time, talents, or finances for you? How did that affect your friendship?
- How do the actions in this story challenge you in your relationship with Jesus?
- What do you need to sacrifice for a friend right now?

Jesus, I apologize for the times that I stay in my comfort zone instead of giving sacrificially to help someone. Thank You for the ultimate sacrifice You offered when You died on the cross. Make me more like You, Jesus, in my willingness to give to others. Amen.

DAY 21
Dirty Job

Washing the Disciples' Feet

O═► BECOME A SERVANT

And since I, your Lord and Teacher, have washed your feet,
you ought to wash each other's feet.

John 13:14

Read John 13:1-17.

I hate taking out the trash. With a fiery, burning passion.

When my sister and I were kids, we had daily chores like most people did. When it was my week to take out the trash, I switched jobs with her so I could clean the kitchen instead. Trash duty takes about six minutes maybe. Kitchen duty takes fifteen minutes every night, but for me, it was totally worth it if I could avoid coming in contact with the trash.

Trash duty meant seeing people's trash—knowing the contents of people's medicine cabinets, the brand of shampoo they used and when they ran out, how much hair was stuck in their shower drain, and how often the women in the house cried at sappy commercials. It grossed me out. Even now, I still hate collecting the trash in my house. I know—First World problem for sure—but I have no qualms about doing other unglamorous chores. I love all the people who make that trash, but somehow, it still makes me want to do dishes instead.

I think it is because trash is just so...dirty. And icky. It takes humility and putting aside my pride (and sense of smell) long enough to serve the others in the house by getting rid of the garbage.

When Jesus washed the feet of His disciples, it was a revolutionary act of humility—but it was also gross. Really gross. It was not like the footbaths in nail salons today, with the massage features, colored lights, and soapy bubbles. It involved twelve men who spent their days walking on dusty, filthy roads in thin sandals. And Jesus, the Son of God, took the time to wash all the muck off of their smelly, dirty feet.

Dis-gust-ing.

Why did He do it? Because their feet were dirty? Well, sure they were dirty, but washing their feet was so much more meaningful than a simple footbath. It was a living parable of sorts. The greatest serving the least. The King serving His followers. The Creator of dust wiping dust from men's feet.

At first, Peter was hesitant. He understood the significance of this act. But when Jesus laid out the ultimatum, Peter jumped in with both feet, so to speak. (Yes, corn-y joke.) I cannot imagine how humbling it must have been for this group of men—who had seen Jesus heal the sick, drive out demons, feed thousands, raise the dead, give sight to the blind, cure leprosy, and calm the waters of the sea—to allow Him to wash their feet, an act usually reserved for the lowliest of servants.

I cannot imagine being Judas, already feeling tempted to betray Jesus and then having that same man wash the filth from my feet in an act of love. And what strength of character in Jesus to wash Judas's feet. Talk about unconditional love!

Let's ruminate on that for a minute. Jesus knew Judas would betray him. He knew that Judas would trade His safety for silver. But He washed Judas's feet anyway. His filthy, stinky, betraying feet. One of the few who saw Jesus heal the sick, give sight to the blind, raise the dead, and feed multitudes threw Jesus to a pack of religious wolves. And yet, Jesus served him by washing his feet anyway.

> **The next time I feel wronged... I need to remember the way that Jesus treated Judas.**

The next time I feel wronged—a political post that makes me mad, a person who cuts me off in traffic, an unkind opinion on one of my social media posts, or someone who makes a joke about my football team—I need to remember the way that Jesus treated Judas. I need to recall how the perfect Son of God humbled Himself to serve a bunch of imperfect humans. Jesus was willing to do the unsavory to show His love. And I need to keep this mindset the next time I face the need to take out the trash.

For Reflection and Prayer

- Have you ever had your feet washed by someone else, perhaps at a retreat or special service? What was that experience like?
- Think about the people you would serve without a second thought. Why is humbling yourself easy to do?
- Who are some people you'd rather not serve? What makes it difficult to be humble around them?

Jesus, You modeled humility when You washed the disciples' feet. You served others even though You deserved to be served. Give me the desire and willingness to follow Your example by serving others, even when it is inconvenient and unsavory. For your glory, Jesus. Amen.

DAY 22
Holy Interruptions

The Hemorrhaging Woman on the Road

🔑 CHANGE YOUR PLANS

When the woman realized that she could not stay hidden,
she began to tremble and fell to her knees in front of him. The
whole crowd heard her explain why she had touched him and
that she had been immediately healed. "Daughter," he said to
her, "your faith has made you well. Go in peace."

Luke 8:47-48

Read Luke 8:42b-48.

My family have a nonverbal signal at our house. It signifies that one member of the household is on the phone. But more than that, it symbolizes the need for the other parties witnessing said signal to not interrupt.

It is a simple signal—the pointer finger. Originally thought to mean "one minute," it means something different in our household. We are talkers. "One" minute could mean one hour, one day, or the time it takes to read all of a Tolkien series. A pointer finger in the air says "Hang on until I get off the phone."

I do not like to be interrupted. Most of the time, it is because I can have the attention span of a gnat and interruptions take me off course. It takes humility to be interrupted and handle it graciously, which I do not always do.

Sandwiched between two parts of an amazing story of Jesus raising Jairus's daughter back to life is one of my favorite parts of Scripture. I know—some people say you're not supposed to have favorites, but this story is more powerful than any Marvel movie. It is fueled solely by God's power and Jesus's willingness to be interrupted.

Jesus was headed to Jairus's house presumably to heal his daughter. Jesus had important work to do. Literally and figuratively, it was a life-and-death situation.

The crowds were so thick and eager to get close to Jesus that verse 42b (NIV) says, "The crowds almost crushed Him."

But there was a woman who was desperate to get close to Jesus. She had heard He had powers to heal. She had suffered from a bleeding disorder for twelve years, which, according to levitical law, meant she was unclean—as was anyone she touched. She was desperate; she had exhausted all the medical treatments she could find and endured physical pain and social rejection. She was probably hoping to slip in unnoticed because she had no other options.

Maybe that is why she came up behind Him. She had a responsibility to avoid contact with others, and yet she was there in the mosh pit in great need of Jesus's attention. She didn't even try to touch Him; she just touched the hem of His garment, and she was immediately healed.

What Jesus did next is so epic. He asked who touched Him (v. 45). First of all, the crowd was so thick that everyone had the capability and access to Jesus, but He knew that healing power had left Him. And because He is all-knowing, He knew who had touched Him. So why did Jesus call attention to the woman? Why not just let her go on her way, healed of her ailment and able to reconnect with others? Because Jesus wanted to restore her heart and her soul, not just her body.

Realizing she couldn't just walk away, the woman finally confessed, trembling with fear. She knew she could be in great trouble for touching Jesus, but she also knew that she had been healed. She proclaimed the miracle "in the presence of all the people" (v. 47 NIV).

Then Jesus said something remarkable: He called her "daughter." After years of living in anonymity, socially ostracized, and forbidden to worship at the synagogue, this woman heard that simple but precious word spoken over her. How that one word must have washed over her parched soul. Jesus then affirmed her faith and sent her on her way in peace.

> **Friends care more about the needs of others and care less about staying on schedule.**

At no time did Jesus signal to anyone there that He was too busy to heal her. He did not seem perturbed at the interruption. He never gave any sign to the crowd or His disciples that He did not want to be disturbed. On the contrary, He stopped to connect with this woman; He saw the moment for what it was: a holy interruption. He chose to alter His agenda to show a desperate woman how valuable she was in the eyes of God.

I need to follow Jesus's example the next time I get frustrated when someone interrupts me. Rather than looking at my watch when a friend needs to talk, I need to remember that Jesus was willing to stop and care for this woman who literally drained Him. Friends care more about the needs of others and care less about staying on schedule. What good will it profit a woman to finish her to-do list but lose her friends in the process?

For Reflection and Prayer

- On a grading scale from A to F, how well do you handle interruptions? More important, how would your family and friends grade you on handling interruptions well?

- Ask God to bring holy interruptions into your day, that is, unexpected opportunities to help a friend (or even a stranger).
- Thank God that you never interrupt Him, that you can always come to Him, day or night.

God, I know I get frustrated by interruptions. Help me see them as holy opportunities to show people how much You value them. I am busy, Lord, but help me never get so busy that I don't take the time to draw others to You. Amen.

DAY 23
Never Too Late

Jairus and His Daughter

O━┳ SEE WITH EYES OF HOPE

After the crowd was put outside, however, Jesus went in and took the girl by the hand, and she stood up!

Matthew 9:25

Read Matthew 9:18-19, 23-26.

As a teenager, I went through a rebellious stage—well, not just a stage, you might say it was the whole theater! I made poor choice upon poor choice and hung out with friends who affirmed my foolishness. It was a prodigal season for me, and I was enjoying the pig slop.

One very late night, my friends and I stopped at a convenience store for food. Our loud and raucous voices filled the small store. The old lady behind the counter did not seem fazed by our volume or the foul language we skillfully used. We loaded up on junk food and headed to the counter. One by one, she graciously rang up each of my friends, smiling at each one. When it was my turn, I did not want to make eye contact with her. Something about her made me very aware of how low my shirt was cut and how badly I had behaved in the store. She announced my total and as soon as I looked her in the eye, she smiled and said, "Jesus loves you."

For some reason her kindness and care made me mad. I made a gesture that would offend a sailor, paid for my snacks, and got back in the car. I was shaking. Her kindness made me look at my current choices, and I did not like what I saw. At first, I thought she had judged me, but the more I thought about it, I was judging me; I knew what I was doing was wrong. Although I continued my shenanigans for a while, I eventually left that friend group, got a new set of friends, and never forgot the old lady who worked the graveyard shift at a convenience store and showed kindness to me.

Sometimes, when people seem to operate without a moral compass, others view them as a lost cause; they are too far gone. They seem too poor, too angry, too drugged up, too broken, too beaten, or too addicted. Fortunately, Jesus does not operate this way.

The man in this story (called Jairus in the other Gospels) was a leader in the synagogue, a very pious dude. But his piety could not save his daughter, nor could his position of authority.

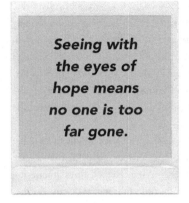

Seeing with the eyes of hope means no one is too far gone.

Many of the disciples may have looked at this man as too far gone—too close to the religious faith of the Pharisees who were trying to kill Jesus. But Jesus saw him with eyes of hope.

The people mourning for this girl thought she was too far gone. She was dead, and you can't fix dead (unless you're the Son of God, of course). The noisy crowd laughed when Jesus suggested she was only sleeping. But Jesus saw her with eyes of hope.

Seeing with the eyes of hope means no one is too far gone. No one is so unlovable, so lost, so broken, that love cannot heal her.

Jairus was looking through the eyes of hope. He knew his daughter was dead, but he also knew that if Jesus would come and put His hand on her, she would live (v. 18). He knew that with Jesus, no one is ever too far gone.

Jesus took her by the hand (v. 25) and looked at her with eyes of hope. Jesus raised her from the dead. As the news of this miracle spread throughout the region (v. 26), people learned that no one is too far gone when Jesus steps in.

One Friday evening decades ago, in the middle of the night in Phoenix, Arizona, my life changed. Someone looked at me—with junk food in my hand and foul words in my mouth—through eyes of hope. Although I did not handle it well then, I cannot wait to meet that old woman in Glory someday and thank her for seeing a child in need of help. Just like Jesus saw Jairus and his daughter.

For Reflection and Prayer

- Is there someone in your life you consider too far gone? Ask God to help you see him or her through the eyes of hope.
- Did someone show you love and compassion when you thought you were too far gone? Thank God for them. If possible, call or write them to say thank you.
- Look for opportunities to show someone that she or he is not too far gone to be changed by Jesus.

Father, thank You for seeing me with eyes of hope. Thank You that no one is too far gone for You to redeem through Jesus. Give me eyes to see those around me who need to hear of Your great love for them. Give me opportunities to tell them. Amen.

DAY 24
Raising and Praising

Mary Magdalene and the Other Mary

O—🔑 SHARE THE MESSAGE

Then the angel spoke to the women. "Don't be afraid!" he said. "I know you are looking for Jesus, who was crucified. He isn't here! He is risen from the dead, just as he said would happen. Come, see where his body was lying."

Matthew 28:5-6

Read Matthew 28:1-10.

When my sister was born, I was just shy of four years old. At that time, hospital protocol kept the mother and the newborn in the hospital for several days. Now, it is more like, "You've already been here three hours. Time to go home."

My dad thought it would be wonderful to surprise my mother by refinishing the rocking chair they had purchased when I was born. It had already been in use for a zillion hours of rocking—to soothe a crying child, to nurse, to read bedtime stories. It needed a fresh coat of varnish and some attention, and my dad saw to it. It was beautiful, but it was supposed to be a secret.

All the way to the hospital to visit my mom and new baby sister, my dad explained the importance of a secret and why I should not, under any circumstances, tell my mom what he had done. I needed to hold that information in my heart and not share it with my mouth.

When I finally got to see my mom and my new sister on the monitor screen at the hospital, my dad covered the microphone for a moment and whispered a reminder: "Please do not tell Mom the secret." I nodded in agreement. But as soon as my dad's hands were off the microphone, I burst forth with the good news. It was a very long time before my dad trusted me with a secret again.

When Jesus rose from the dead, it should not have been a secret or a surprise to His followers. He had told them about it several times and in various ways, but they did not seem to get it. When He died, they lost all hope.

On that early morning, Mary Magdalene and the other Mary (I wish we knew her full name) were the first to receive the good news of Jesus's resurrection. They didn't just hear about

Him; they saw Him with their own eyes. They were the first eye-witnesses to the greatest event in history.

When I was in Bible college, some friends and I were talking about the gender roles in the New Testament and the pervasive culture at the time. We decided it was an interesting choice for Jesus to appear to women first, since the word of a woman did not hold weight in a court of law. A friend in the room who was dedicated to women's rights said, "See, this just proves that Jesus supported equality." One of the other women in the room responded, "Yes, but He also knew if He gave the message to women, it would get around faster!"

Although we all burst into laughter, we knew that such a reputation is a stereotype many women fight—but in my case, as a talker, it's one I might exacerbate!

Stereotypes aside, I love that Jesus saw past the cultural limitations of the day and appeared to two of His faithful female followers. I am certain the ladies weren't thinking about the significance of Jesus's appearing to them first. I think they were overcome with excitement, fear, shock, and hope, among many other emotions. I know I would have been!

> **You and I have the opportunity to tell our friends about the One who gave His life for them.**

Jesus entrusted them with the good news to share. He gives you and me the same assignment today. You and I have the opportunity to tell our friends about the One who gave His life for them. We get to tell others that, despite their sin, God loves them. We get to tell others that death has no victory because Jesus conquered death with life. Like the women centuries ago, you and I get to tell the world, "He is risen from the dead" (v. 6).

That's the best news we could ever share with our friends. And we never, ever have to keep it a secret.

For Reflection and Prayer

- Think of someone you know who needs to know how much God loves him or her—someone who seems lonely or isolated, who is going through a difficult season, or someone from whom you have not heard in a while. Pray for the opportunity to tell this person about what God offers him or her through Jesus.
- Why do you think people keep their faith a secret? What keeps you from telling others about what you believe?
- Ask God to give you courage and boldness to talk about your faith.

God, the resurrection of Your Son is no secret. It's the greatest news ever. May I be unafraid to tell others about Jesus. Give me favor with others so they will be drawn to the Truth. Amen.

DAY 25
Shore Thing

Jesus Makes the Disciples Breakfast

O━━┳ CONNECT OVER FOOD

When they got there, they found breakfast waiting for them—
fish cooking over a charcoal fire, and some bread.

John 21:9

Read John 21:1-14.

I have a carrot cake recipe that is so good, it will make you give extra when the offering plate is passed at church. I have actually won "church throwdown" competitions with it! Nothing says biblical community like bloodthirsty, competitive, baking Christians!

Throughout the Bible, food is used to connect, celebrate, and nourish. Although some of us can be guilty of overeating and using food as a comfort and a crutch, Jesus set an example throughout the Scriptures by using food to draw people together. He ate dinner with tax collectors and "sinners" (Matthew 9:10). He multiplied fish and bread to feed thousands of people (Matthew 14:13-21). He joined two men for dinner after traveling with them on the road to Emmaus (Luke 24:28-32). And He provided food for the disciples after a failed fishing excursion (John 21:1-14).

After the Resurrection, Peter decided to go fishing. (We all like to go back to what's familiar when our world feels upside-down.) Some of the other disciples went along, including James and John, who had also been fishermen before they had become fishers of men. Despite their vast experience and technique, the men caught nothing. Unknown to them, Jesus had walked onto the shore. He called out to the disciples and told them to cast their nets in a different place.

Holy mackerel (or carp or tilapia), what a load of fish they caught! Jesus had provided so many fish to catch, the nets were filled to capacity—153 large fish—and yet the nets didn't break! (I've always wondered who counted them. And who remembered that number so many years later when the Gospel of John was written?)

When John told Peter it was Jesus on the shore, Peter jumped into the water to swim to Him. When the disciples all arrived, there was a fire waiting for them (v. 9). Jesus had been cooking breakfast for the tired and undoubtedly hungry men.

The last time Jesus and Peter had an intimate conversation, Jesus was predicting that Peter would betray Him three times before the rooster crowed (meaning the next morning), to which Peter adamantly denied he would. And then after Jesus was taken into custody by the religious leaders, Peter denied Jesus three times, standing by a fire (Mark 14:66-72). Now he was sitting by the fire with Jesus, whom he had betrayed. Ouch. But Jesus used the occasion to restore Peter and give him a mission and a purpose.

I rarely think of Jesus just hanging out and enjoying the company of others, but that is exactly what He did in these verses. He fed the disciples (which always makes me feel better). He connected with them. I imagine He told a few stories over that fire. And after breakfast, He brought Peter to a new level of trust and obedience.

As the followers of Christ, we should not underestimate the power of a simple meal and an exchange filled with grace. I have had lots of meetings at a coffee shop where a muffin and a latte were shared and ideas were exchanged. There have been family dinners where my clan has poured into and prayed for one another. Holy moments in my life have not been limited to church buildings but sometimes have happened when believers have acted as the church and loved others well by bringing a meal when our family was in need. Eating together can be an opportunity to get to know others, hear their stories, share struggles and triumphs, and experience the power of connection with people who are journeying with us on the path of faith.

Recently, a man from our church had some really scary heart issues. When he and his wife returned home after weeks in the hospital, my husband and I took a meal to them. Not wanting to be a bother, we planned to drop off the meal, pray for them, and leave. But the wife had other plans. "Come and eat with us," she said. "The fellowship is the most filling part, no matter how good the meal is."

> **We should not underestimate the power of a simple meal and an exchange filled with grace.**

Jesus broke bread with His disciples on the shore; He filled their bellies with food and their hearts with the assurance of God's love. Let us do likewise.

For Reflection and Prayer

- Who in your life could use the encouragement of a simple connection time with you?
- Who would you like to connect with?
- When was the last time you connected with God and His Word? Set aside time in your schedule to enjoy Jesus's company.

Father, I need You. I need Your provision, Your forgiveness, and Your grace. Help me to connect with others well because I need the encouragement, the wisdom, and the joy that others bring into my life. I love You, Lord. Amen.

DAY 26
Food Network

Reclining at the Table

O━━ JUST HANG OUT

When the time came, Jesus and the apostles sat down together at the table.

Luke 22:14

Read Luke 22:14.

My mom used an expression for those who did not have a lot of mental acuity. She would say they "could not walk and chew gum at the same time."

I can do that easily. I can walk, chew gum, grocery shop, make a pizza, and talk to someone on the phone all at once. I am a marvel of multitasking. Except when I am typing. I cannot type and listen to someone talk at the same time. If someone is having a conversation with me and I am typing something, some of their words end up in my document. My family thinks this is hilarious.

One time, I got up early to answer the 127 emails in my inbox. One of those was from a friend who shared with me that she was going through a rough time. I was really touched by her email and wanted to respond with the most comforting words I know: Psalm 23. I have it memorized, so I began to type it from memory, when my family entered the kitchen and started talking about breakfast. I tried not to listen to their conversation, but I found myself thinking about omelets and pancakes. I finished the email to my hurting friend, but I read through it one more time to make sure there were no apparent errors in punctuation, grammar, or spelling. I am so thankful I did. While my family was discussing all the wonderful choices for breakfast, one of their suggestions made it into my email inadvertently: "The Lord is my bacon, I shall not want."

Oh my. I told you I cannot be trusted with a keyboard when people are talking! I would have confused my friend and confessed my food idolatry all at the same time.

Multitasking is sometimes a necessity in these busy times, but I think the quality of our work suffers when we focus on more than one task at a time. Unlike people in today's world, Jesus was intentional with His connections with people and the time they spent together.

In this part of the gospel story, Jesus knew that He would be betrayed and killed. He knew that one of His own followers, a man who had witnessed all the miracles, who had been a part of unexplainable wonders, and who had walked with Jesus every day, was going to betray Him. He knew He would suffer under the cruelty of Roman punishment.

In these last moments with His disciples, He could have preached a sermon series. He could have performed more wonders, healed more sick folks, fed more crowds, and raised more dead people. But He didn't. On the night Jesus was betrayed, He chose to hang out with His people.

They were reclining at the table—a hard concept to grasp in the twenty-first century. But the tables at that time were part table and part sofa, structured to provide a connecting place as much as a place to eat. (I am ready for La-Z-Boy to create something like that.) In biblical times, friends and family would even recline on one another as they talked and ate. (I'd probably spill something on someone!) Meals were more relaxed and lasted longer than today's meals. And sharing a meal was a sign of relationship. To invite someone into your home was an invitation to friendship.

> **We could all benefit from being in the present moment, being still, and being together with no agenda other than friendship.**

The disciples were just hanging out with Jesus. And He with them. No doubt He had a lot on

111

His mind, but He chose to take the time to just be—be present, be still, be together. In today's frenetic world where productivity trumps everything else, we could all benefit from being in the present moment, being still, and being together with no agenda other than friendship.

Quality relationships cannot be rushed. They're more like a delicious meal cooked slowly on a grill or stovetop than a frozen dinner zapped in a microwave. Good relationships simply cannot be "cooked"—forged and matured—quickly. They are made with a lot of quality time, with the spices of shared hardship and celebration thrown in. And most important, Jesus's example is the guiding recipe!

For Reflection and Prayer

- When was the last time you put everything else aside to enjoy the company of a friend? What was that encounter like?
- What distractions can you remove so you can focus on the people you are with (turn off the TV, put away your phone, and so on)?

Father, forgive me for the times I am busy with tasks and focused on activity instead of connecting with others. Thank You for Jesus's example of being present and available to others. May I slow down long enough today to really enjoy the people You put in my path. Amen.

DAY 27
Service with a Smile

Mary and Martha

"Martha, Martha," the Lord answered, "you are worried and upset about many things, but few things are needed—or indeed only one."

Luke 10:41-42 NIV

Read Luke 10:38-42.

My husband had childhood friends who could not be trusted with popcorn because they would snort the kernels up their noses.

My sister got a Hot Wheels car tire stuck in her nose when we were growing up.

What is it about kids and items in our noses?

When British youngster Steve Easton was only seven years old, he snorted the suction part of a toy dart up his nose. Medical professionals never found anything in the boy's nasal passages, but for decades, he suffered with headaches and sniffles. Almost four decades after the initial incident and a very strong sneeze, the toy part came out of his left nostril.[1] Talk about unresolved childhood issues.

You're welcome. I know that story just blesses your heart.

Much like the man with the dart in his nose (yes, I brought it up again—no pun intended; just kidding, I love puns—totally intended), Martha had some unresolved issues. I empathize with her. She tried to help Jesus by opening her house to Him, along with His disciples. She was a little flustered and questioned Jesus. Yep. She did. She asked the Son of God, the Word made flesh, and the Alpha and Omega, if He even cared about the current situation. Yowza. Holy guts, Batman. It is clear that she felt overlooked, underappreciated, and isolated. She spoke to Jesus with a tone I imagine sounded a lot like a teenager. In my head, I hear the Valley girl accent I used as a teenager when I read, "Lord, don't you care [overlooked] that my sister has left me to do the work [underappreciated] by myself [isolated]? Tell her to help me!" (v. 40 NIV, additions mine).

---

1 "Camberley Man, 51, Sneezes Out Childhood Toy Dart End," *BBC News*, May 12, 2015, https://www.bbc.com/news/uk-england-surrey-32710540, accessed December 11, 2020.

Such indignation had probably been brewing under the surface for some time, likely coming from years of overextending in the name of good intentions (or cultural norms). Verse 40 indicates that she thought no one saw the hard work she had put in, and she was incensed

Connecting sometimes involves helping people deal with unresolved issues.

that Mary hadn't lifted a finger. Or maybe those are just my issues that I am projecting on a woman born two thousand years before me.

But Jesus was not offended by her indignation. He did not repay in kind or start a contest about whose life was more difficult. Instead, He called her by name, twice, maybe to get her attention or to make sure she knew she was seen. He knew that she was speaking out of hurt, so He chose to respond in kindness, in patience, and in redirection.

Jesus's actions illustrate an important point: connecting sometimes involves helping people deal with unresolved issues.

Sometimes when dealing with others, unresolved issues can poison connection. Unless we deal with our personal struggles,

115

our own brokenness from the past can begin to chip away at the relationships in our present. Jesus did not allow Martha's hurts to create a barrier between them. Instead, He named the problem and helped her move beyond it. He loved her where she was, but He also loved her enough to not let her stay in the hurt. That's what good friends do.

And that's what you and I are called to do too.

There is an old adage that "hurt people hurt people." I have seen that play itself out in my life for sure. But what about the idea that "loved people love people"? When I am in God's Word regularly and therefore reminded consistently of His great love for me, my emotional and spiritual accounts have more to draw from when I am interacting with others.

The Scriptures encourage us, "Praise be to the God and Father of our Lord Jesus Christ, the Father of compassion and the God of all comfort, who comforts us in all our troubles, so that we can comfort those in any trouble with the comfort we ourselves receive from God" (2 Corinthians 1:3-4 NIV). So, maybe another saying should be "comforted people comfort people."

Throughout God's Word, you and I are called to love, heal, teach, comfort, support, admonish, and care for others—out of the account balances we have received from God.

Jesus set this example with Martha. And you and I can do it every day with those whom God places in our paths: people with issues; people like us.

For Reflection and Prayer

- In your life, who has loved you enough to help you confront issues that were weighing you down?
- Ask God to show you any relationships that may be hurting from unresolved issues.
- Thank God for loving you so much that He wants you to grow beyond your past.

God, I praise You for being a God who truly sees me and loves me anyway. You are well aware of my past hurts—You were there when others hurt me and when I hurt others—and You call me to a future of hope and healing. Help me to offer that to others. Help me not to be hurtful when others offend me, but instead to repay unkindness with love. Amen.

DAY 28
Unlikely Hero

The Good Samaritan

⚷—┳ LOVE INDISCRIMINATELY

"'Now which of these three would you say was a neighbor to the man who was attacked by bandits?" Jesus asked.

The man replied, "The one who showed him mercy."

Then Jesus said, "Yes, now go and do the same."

Luke 10:36-37

Read Luke 10:25-37.

Both of our kids played instruments in elementary school. Our daughter played the clarinet and our son played the trombone. They both had excellent teachers who fostered excitement for music in students, but when those teachers no longer had an influence in the lives of our kids, both lost their excitement quickly.

After many years of instruments, supplies, time, and lessons, we had invested a significant amount. We decided that since both kids were uninterested in continuing to play their respective instruments, we would sell them.

We have a thriving online community in our area. People are always buying and selling things, and I knew that someone would be excited about the prospect of snagging an instrument at a lower cost. Discounts make clothes fit better, cars run better, and instruments sound better.

I placed the ad, and like most of the ads on the site I was using, I included the abbreviation "OBO" after the price, which means "or best offer." I am a professional bargain hunter. I have known OBO since I could walk (okay, not really, but as long as I could walk to a garage sale). Thrift runs deep in my blood, and I consider my savvy at a garage sale a spiritual gift.

The clarinet went right away; it is a very popular instrument for beginners. The trombone, on the other hand, was harder to sell.

But I finally received a message in my inbox. I opened it excitedly, only to find that the person misunderstood the ad. "How much for the OBOE?"

Ugh.

When an expert in the Law approached Jesus in Luke 10, the man was attempting to test Him. Jesus navigated the test by asking the man a series of questions, affirming his knowledge of the Law, and then He told a story to articulate His point.

119

The story He told is one of the most recognized in the entire New Testament. You may know it well. Even in secular circles, this story often is referred to when someone shows kindness to another. Hospitals have been named after the protagonist in this story!

Jesus told the parable of the good Samaritan in response to this question from a lawyer: "Who is my neighbor?" (Luke 10:29b). The parable is about a traveling man who was beaten, stripped of his clothing, and left to die alongside the road on his way to Jericho from Jerusalem. Both a priest and a Levite (religious leader) saw him, but they chose to cross the road on the other side and ignore the suffering man. Finally, a Samaritan happened upon the traveler. The Samaritans and Jews were enemies, but despite the cultural divide, the Samaritan helped the injured man, transported him to care, and paid for him to be doctored (Luke 10:25-37).

When Jesus started talking about the Samaritan, the expert in the Law must have heard something like the "Imperial March" from *Star Wars* in his head. Samaritans were the sworn enemies of the Jews, so seeing a Samaritan as the good guy in the story must have been mind-blowing for the expert. When Jesus asked the man to identify the "neighbor," the man couldn't even say the word *Samaritan* in a positive light. Instead, he used the phrase, "The one who showed him mercy" (v. 37). I picture him saying it through gritted teeth, like a teenager who hates to admit his parents were right.

The expert in the Law, much like the person inquiring about the ad for the trombone, misunderstood what the Law meant. Loving your neighbor doesn't have limits based on property lines. It doesn't have limits based on political affiliation, gender, religion, or a favorite sports team. We don't love people because they think, act, or look like we do. We love others because God loves us (1 John 4:19). It has always been about love (Matthew 22:37–40). When we put conditions on who we care about and who deserves to be loved, we misunderstand the heart of God.

> **We are not called to a life of simplicity but, instead, to a life of obedience, which means we are to love all people.**

Is it easier to love people like us? You bet it is! It is simpler perhaps, yet we are not called to a life of simplicity but, instead, to a life of obedience, which means we are to love all people. God has planned for you and me to grow in our likeness of His Son, and the growth accelerant He often uses is interpersonal relationships, especially the ones that challenge us.

In this passage, Jesus gives us the two greatest commandments: "He answered, 'Love the Lord your God with all your heart and with all your soul and with all your strength and with all your mind'; and, 'Love your neighbor as yourself'" (Luke 10:27 NIV).

God commands it, Jesus models it, and the parable of the good Samaritan illustrates how we can live it—even with those with whom we do not agree.

For Reflection and Prayer

- Think of someone in your life whom you struggle to love. Ask God to give you compassion and love from His heart.
- Whom have you dismissed because she or he doesn't think, act, or look like you? Ask God to show you how to repair that relationship if possible. Seek out forgiveness from that person.

Father, forgive me for basing my love for others on human criteria. Forgive me for mistreating others because they are different than I am. Help me follow the example of Jesus in my interactions with others, showing love and compassion because they are Your beloved children. Help me glorify You in the way I treat others. Amen.

DAY 29
Marching Orders

Jesus Sends Out the Seventy-two

O━━ TRUST IN GOD'S PROVISION

These were his instructions to them: "The harvest is great, but the workers are few. So pray to the Lord who is in charge of the harvest; ask him to send more workers into his fields."

Luke 10:2

Read Luke 10:1-9.

I do not like practical jokes. They often have a malicious intent, cause dissension, foster hurt feelings, and encourage revenge.

That being said, one April Fools' Day, my sister and I decided to play a trick on our beloved mother. She is a faithful coffee drinker. She used to get up hours before she needed to leave so she could sit on our patio, drink her coffee, and collect her thoughts before she had to face a substantial commute, stressful workloads, and the challenges of leadership.

Often, if one of us would walk in the backyard to see her, she would ask for us to refill her coffee. On this April Fools' Day, I went out to make small talk (more like unintelligible mumbling, since we're not morning people), and she nicely asked me to refill her coffee.

When I opened the door, my sister sprang into action. She grabbed the soy sauce from our refrigerator, and we filled the cup. We then threw it in the microwave (to heat it up a bit), giggling all the way. As soon as it warmed up, I returned the cup to my mom.

She grabbed the cup and took a swig before the pungent smell of soy sauce had the opportunity to warn her. My mom did a spit take. At an early hour of the morning, our sweet mom spewed the contents of her mouth all over the patio.

Watching from the window, my sister and I laughed at first. We howled. We hooted. And then we saw her. Soy sauce dripping from her lips and disappointment on her face.

Our laughter stopped. I grabbed a towel and my sister grabbed another cup of coffee. We went outside and hugged our mom and apologized for such a cruel gag. She forgave us and then charged us with the responsibility of cleaning up the patio. (Now that I am the mom who drinks coffee every morning, I hope my kids never read this and get any funny ideas.)

When Jesus sent out seventy-two newly appointed ambassadors, some of His instructions must have felt like an

April Fools' joke. "Now go, and remember that I am sending you out as lambs among wolves" (v. 3). I would have raised my hand and asked for clarification. "No purse? No extra sandals? No provisions? I'm sure I misunderstood you, Jesus."

Jesus wanted His followers to trust God for their needs. He offered them the power they needed to accomplish the mission. He warned them that not everyone would be receptive to this message and that as His followers, their job was to extend peace anyway. Many who saw Jesus in the flesh did not grasp Who He was or what His purpose was, but He loved them despite their lack of receptivity.

Those same instructions can encourage all of us who want to make a difference for Christ. The same Spirit that raised Jesus from the dead is available to us (Romans 8:11). We can trust God for our needs. And like the early disciples' experience, not everyone will accept our message. In fact, some people will be downright mean. We can extend grace and peace anyway.

> **Relationships born out of obedience might develop into friendships that bless us beyond measure.**

However, some people will accept our message. When we are faithful to live and love the gospel in our interactions, our words, and our prayers, we don't know how we might affect others. We don't know what relationships will develop out of our obedience to "go" and "trust." We don't know how those relationships born out of obedience might develop into friendships that bless us beyond measure.

The fields are still ready for the harvest. It's up to you and me to fulfill the mission Jesus calls us to complete. The outcome is up to Him. All we have to do is say yes and trust in God's provision.

For Reflection and Prayer

- Where is your harvest field? That is, where has God placed you to be His messenger?
- Ask God to empower you to go outside your comfort zone to tell people about Jesus's love for them.

God, I have the opportunity and honor to take the message of Your love to the world. Let me always be prepared to give an answer for the hope I have in You. Show me how to walk in Your power and strength so You are glorified. Amen.

DAY 30
Name Dropping

Healing of Aeneas and Dorcas

🔑 DO GOOD IN JESUS'S NAME

Peter said to him, "Aeneas, Jesus Christ heals you! Get up, and roll up your sleeping mat!" And he was healed instantly.

Acts 9:34

Read Acts 9:32-42.

When my sister and I were teenagers, she would often perceive things as unfair because I had opportunities and freedoms that she did not. I was almost four years older and we were three years apart in school, but that did not stop her from resenting me a bit.

We were very close. We often shared friends and clothes and secrets. But during one season of our lives, she kept a secret from me.

127

Long before the advanced computer systems we have today, if you had a birth certificate and social security card in the US, you could apply for a driver's license replacement card. Without my knowledge, my sister "borrowed" my documents, entered the closest Motor Vehicle Department, acted like she was me, applied for a replacement license, and had her picture placed on it. For years, when she needed to appear older, she would use that license.

On the occasion of her twenty-first birthday, she gave me that license with her photo on it. She admitted that for years, when it was necessary, she would pretend to be me. She did things in my place, using my name. Fortunately, she never got into trouble. She never got caught. She never besmirched my name. (I did plenty of my own besmirching!)

In Acts 9:32-42, Peter acted in Jesus's name. He encouraged people, he healed a lame man, and he raised a girl from the dead—all in the name of the Son of God. He was operating in the power of God for the glory of God. God worked through him to do amazing things—miracles and wonders—in the name of Jesus.

In these verses, Peter demonstrated a wonderful truth— God uses His people to draw others into relationship with Him. He did incredible things through His disciples, and He will do incredible things through you and me. In fact, Jesus said, "I tell you the truth, anyone who believes in me will do the same works I have done, and even greater works, because I am going to be with the Father" (John 14:12).

Holy Spirit power, Batman! When Jesus sent the Holy Spirit to the early church (Acts 1–2), these believers did what Jesus had done, performing signs and miracles to demonstrate what His Kingdom would be like. People like Peter, Paul, John,

> **You and I have the opportunity to do great things in Jesus's name as His representatives here on earth.**

and Philip (among many others) did things in Jesus's name. And God wants to use you and me, too.

You and I have the opportunity to do great things in Jesus's name as His representatives here on earth. Every believer has been given gifts to build up the church and to bring glory to God. It's never about us or making a name for ourselves; it's about pointing people to Christ, who died for them so they can have an eternal relationship with God that begins here and now. His name—and His fame—is the only one that matters.

Even if no one knows us, learns our names, or gets our names right once they do know us, we are Jesus by proxy in a lost world. Although He gives us the desire, the purpose, the power, and the opportunity to share Christ with those with whom we come in contact, we are the ones who have to heed His call. Like an Olympic runner carrying the torch to represent his or her country, we take the light of Christ to a dark world. What an honor. What a responsibility. What a gift. And what a difference God can make through us in the life of another. Like Peter, let us do good in Jesus's name!

For Reflection and Prayer

- How has God uniquely gifted you to point others to Him?
- What might it look like for you to live and act in the power of the Holy Spirit?
- Who is a role model of living by the power of the Spirit?

Father, please forgive me for the times I make things about me. I want to forge friendships in Your name for Your glory. I want to live in the power of Your Spirit so I can point people to You. Amen.

DAY 31
True Love

"For God So Loved . . ."

🔑 LOVE OTHERS

"For God so loved the world that he gave his one and only Son, that whoever believes in him shall not perish but have eternal life. For God did not send his Son into the world to condemn the world, but to save the world through him."

John 3:16-17 NIV

Read John 3:16-17.

This thirty-one-day journey has been designed to help you see how Jesus dealt with people with whom He came in contact. How He responded to the hurting, the defensive, the mistreated, and the outcasts can provide a road map for us to do likewise.

When Scott and I were first married, we were serving in a ministry in Southern California. There are a few things you come to expect in such a place: the weather is beautiful, the real estate is expensive, and the traffic is horrible. Sometimes, it would take hours to travel a few miles—and not just during rush hour.

It was about this time in California history when a series of drive-by shootings occurred. They were seemingly random, many of the victims were strangers to the shooters, and road rage was often the culprit. People can get really crazy in traffic…but enough about me.

On a warm summer day, I had borrowed my husband's car and I headed to Los Angeles (where many of these shootings had occurred). The traffic stopped completely. People in the cars around me grew impatient and most of us turned off our car engines to save gas. As the minutes ticked by, the temperature rose and tempers flared from the drivers on either side of me. I could feel a panic growing inside—not because of the traffic, but because I was afraid of being shot and taking my last breaths on the 405.

Then it happened—the moment I had most feared. I heard a loud pop from behind me. I felt a warm ooze soak through my clothing. After some quick prayers and a few tears, I reached down to assess the damage to my body. I was not in pain, but when I touched my blouse, I realized my blood was clear. I have watched way too much CSI in my day, so I went through a few scenarios in my head.

Then I smelled the blood (I know, ewww). It smelled…like citrus.

I didn't know this at the time, but my husband had a few

sodas in the back seat of the car. One of them must have received direct sunlight for too long and it exploded, spewing clear, citrusy goodness all over the headliner of the car, my hair, and my clothing.

I hadn't been shot. I had been Sprite-ed.

But the whole ordeal gave me a lot to think about, and the traffic on the freeway ensured I had plenty of time to think. What if that *had* been my last day on earth? How would I be remembered? How did I treat people? Did I show people how much Jesus loves them?

When Jesus came to earth, He set the perfect example of how to interact with others, even for those who would be born centuries later.

"For God so loved the world that he gave his one and only Son, that whoever believes in him shall not perish but have eternal life. For God did not send his Son into the world to condemn the world, but to save the world through him" (John 3:16-17 NIV).

He initiated the relationship with the world—and with you and me.

He sacrificed to make the relationship work.

He gave (and continues to do so) because of love. For relationship.

How can we begin a Friendship Initiative that far exceeds thirty-one days, but instead, becomes a daily practice that makes an eternal difference? By doing what Jesus did. By loving. By sacrificing. By challenging cultural and religious biases. Just as Jesus did what He saw His Father doing (John 5:19-20), you and

Let's love the people God places in our path.

I can follow in Jesus's footsteps by doing what He did.

Thank you for taking this journey with me. Much like my day on the 405, it has given me lots to think about, pray about, and aspire toward. Let's love the people God places in our path and be remembered as people who followed the example of their Savior.

For Reflection and Prayer

- How has God moved in your life throughout this journey?
- How are you different because you encountered Jesus?

Father, thank You for this journey. I pray for Your guidance as I continue to develop friendships. Thank You for initiating a relationship with Your people, sacrificing for them, and always working in their best interests. Grant me the strength to follow Your example. Amen.

A Final Word

I often read devotionals to focus my mind and heart. They serve as an "amuse-bouche" or appetizer—a little taste of how the author has been encouraged by God and how I can learn from his or her journey. My prayer is that these thirty-one days have not simply given you a taste of my journey but have encouraged you to know and love others more following the example of Jesus. I pray you have been challenged to look at the ways He came in contact with others and how those interactions profoundly changed all who encountered Him.

I know you are busy; I am too. But may we never grow so busy that we forget how Jesus initiated a friendship with us. No matter how it happened—whether you grew up in the church, came to a saving knowledge of Jesus as a teen or young adult, or have just recently learned of His great love for you—remember that He was the initiator. God, the Maker of heaven and earth, sent His Son to initiate a relationship with humanity—with you and me. Whether you relate more to Zacchaeus, the adulterous woman, the centurion, Mary, the boy who shared his lunch, Martha, or another character we considered in our journey together, may you know from your messy bun down to your chipped toenail polish just how important you are to Jesus.

You are important enough for Him to die on the cross for you, important enough for Him to initiate a friendship with you, and important enough for Him to ask you to reach out in friendship to others, in His name and for His glory. Let's love with our lives, honor with our hearts, and reach out with our relationships.

Let's begin a friendship initiative with a world that needs more peace, more patience, more kindness, and more grace. Let's smile with more regularity, listen with more intent, pray with more fervor, trust with more abandon, and watch with more attentiveness as God uses our actions to point people to Himself.

God bless you. Thank you for your willingness to learn alongside me. Please let me know if God has challenged you in these thirty-one days and how He has prompted you to creatively love others. I'd love to hear from you (see below for ways to connect).

I am praying for you!

Connect with Amberly:

@amberlyneese

@amberlyneese

@Amberly Neese - Comedian and Speaker

Website   www.amberlyneese.com

Learn to live at peace with others even when you disagree by studying biblical stories of rivalries in *Common Ground* by Amberly Neese.

Common Ground: Loving Others Despite Our Differences

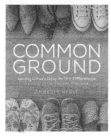

Study Guide with Leader Helps
9781791014506 | $16.99

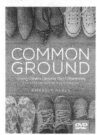

Video-DVD
9781791014520 | $44.99

Whether it is in politics, the professional world, a party, or a pew, we face conflict every day. As discussions get more heated and social media is deluged with opinion-spewing, hurt feelings, and broken relationships, we need hope and practical tools to navigate the tumultuous waters and live at peace with everyone.

Fortunately, the Scriptures hold the key to living at peace despite our differences. In *Common Ground*, a four-week Bible study, Amberly Neese combines stories of sibling rivalries from the Bible with personal experience, humor, hope, and her love of God's Word.

Stories examined from the Old and New Testaments include:
- Joseph and His Brothers: How to Combat Jealousy
- Moses, Miriam, and Aaron: How to Work Together Despite Differences
- Mary, Martha, and Lazarus: How to Appreciate the Contributions of Others
- Rachel and Leah: Having Compassion for the Plight of Others

Explore excerpts and video teaching samples at AbingdonWomen.com.

Made in the USA
Monee, IL
12 March 2022

92803420R00085